Welcome Home

5-INGREDIENT
COOKBOOK

EASY MEALS FOR BUSY LIVES

Hope Comerford

Good Books

New York, New York

Good Books books may be purchased in bulk at special discounts for sales promotion, corporate gifts, fund-raising, or educational purposes. Special editions can also be created to specifications. For details, contact the Special Sales Department, Good Books, 307 West 36th Street, 11th Floor, New York, NY 10018 or info@skyhorsepublishing.com.

Good Books is an imprint of Skyhorse Publishing, Inc.®, a Delaware corporation.

Visit our website at www.goodbooks.com.

10 9 8 7 6 5 4 3 2 1

Library of Congress Cataloging-in-Publication Data is available on file.

Cover design by David Ter-Avanesyan
Cover photos by Meredith Special Interest Media and Bonnie Matthews

Print ISBN: 978-1-68099-787-3
Ebook ISBN: 978-1-68099-833-7

Printed in China

Table of Contents

Welcome to Welcome Home 5-Ingredient Cookbook

Like it or not, we are all living in very busy times. Even at our busiest of times, however, we all still deserve a home-cooked meal! That's where this book steps in! Whether you're looking for a stove-top, oven, slow cooker, or Instant Pot recipe, you will find just what you need, right here in this book. All of the recipes in this book contain five ingredients or less, which require a few pantry staples and a short list of ingredients. A short ingredient list means your grocery list will be a little bit shorter too. It will be easier than ever for you stay on budget when shopping for the recipes in this book!

As always, this book contains recipes you can trust because they are all tried and true, by home cooks like you! You'll find recipes that will please even the pickiest of eaters, without fancy or hard-to-find ingredients. You can cook with confidence when you choose a Welcome Home 5-Ingredient Recipe from this cookbook!

What qualifies as a 5-Ingredient recipe?
- A recipe that has five or fewer ingredients.
- Spices, baking powder, and baking soda do not count.
- Water does not count.
- Oil does not count.
- Optional ingredients do not count.
- Serving suggestion items, such as rice or pasta, do not count.

BREAKFAST & BRUNCH

Sticky Buns

Elaine Rineer, Lancaster, PA

Makes 12 servings

Prep. Time: 20 minutes ❧ *Chilling Time: 8 hours, or overnight* ❧ *Baking Time: 35 minutes*

1 stick (8 Tbsp.) butter, *divided*
½ cup brown sugar
½ cup corn syrup
¼ cup plus 2 Tbsp. sugar
2 Tbsp. cinnamon
2 loaves frozen bread dough, thawed

1. In a saucepan, melt ½ stick (4 Tbsp.) of the butter on stove top or in microwave. Stir in the brown sugar and corn syrup until well blended. Pour into a 9×13-inch baking pan.

2. Melt remaining ½ stick (4 Tbsp.) butter in microwave or on stove top. Set aside.

3. In a small mixing bowl, combine the sugar and cinnamon.

4. Break off golf-ball-sized pieces of bread dough, 12 per loaf. Dip each in melted butter and then roll in the sugar-cinnamon mixture. Place coated balls in baking pan.

5. Cover and refrigerate for 8 hours, or overnight.

6. Remove from the refrigerator and let stand for 30 minutes before baking.

7. Bake uncovered at 325°F for 35 minutes. Turn out of the pan immediately onto a serving platter.

Variation:

Add ½ cup to ¾ cup chopped pecans to mixture in pan (Step 1).

Easy Doughnuts

Monica Yoder, Millersburg, OH

Makes 8 servings

Prep. Time: 10 minutes   ⚘   Cooking/Baking Time: 6 minutes

¾ cup vegetable oil, *divided*
Tube 8 large, refrigerated biscuits
½ cup sugar
¼ tsp. ground cinnamon

1. In a medium skillet over medium-low heat, heat ½ cup of the oil.

2. Use a 1-inch round cookie cutter to cut a hole in the center of each biscuit; reserve the extra dough for "holes."

3. Test the heat of the oil by dipping the edge of a doughnut in the pan. The edge will bubble if the oil is hot enough.

4. Place 4 doughnuts and holes in the skillet and cook until golden brown, about 1 to 1½ minutes on each side. Transfer to a wire rack or paper-towel-lined plate to drain.

5. Add the remaining oil to the skillet and cook the remaining doughnuts and holes.

6. In a large bowl, combine the sugar and cinnamon. Gently toss the warm doughnuts in the mixture, a few at a time. Serve warm or at room temperature.

Tip:

You can also toss the doughnuts in confectioners' sugar.

Crêpes

Norma Grieser, Clarksville, MI

Makes 4–6 servings

Prep. Time: 5 minutes ⚮ *Cooking/Baking Time: 15 minutes*

3 eggs

½ cup milk

¼ cup flour

Pinch salt

2 Tbsp. butter, melted, plus some for greasing skillet

1. In a mixing bowl, use a wire whisk to mix all ingredients together.

2. Grease a skillet with the butter. Heat over medium-high heat.

3. Put 2½ Tbsp. (or just a bit over half of a ¼ cup measure) of the mixture in the hot skillet. Immediately pick up the skillet and let the batter roll around the bottom of the pan to form a thin layer in the skillet. Cook until lightly browned.

4. Flip and cook the other side. You may need to use your fingers to flip the crepes.

5. Remove from the skillet when lightly browned. Spread with maple syrup or your favorite jam. Roll up and enjoy.

Serving suggestion:

Top the rolled-up crêpes with sliced fresh peaches, sprinkled with confectioners' sugar!

Fluffy "Homemade" from the Box Pancakes

Valerie Drobel, Carlisle, PA

Makes 4 servings

Prep. Time: 5 minutes ⚘ *Cooking/Baking Time: 4–6 minutes*

2 cups buttermilk baking mix

2 eggs

1½ cups milk

1 cup ricotta cheese

1 Tbsp. lemon juice

1. In a large mixing bowl, combine all ingredients. Mix until smooth.

2. Lightly oil the surface of a griddle and heat to approximately 350°F or warm a skillet.

3. Pour the batter onto the griddle or into the skillet in 5-inch circles. Cook until bubbly (about 2 to 3 minutes).

4. Flip and cook for 2 minutes more.

Tip:

Add ¾ cup fresh blueberries to Step 1, if you wish.

Fast, Friendly French Toast

Donna Barnitz, Rio Rancho, NM

Makes 4 servings

Prep. Time: 15 minutes ⚬ Soaking Time: 1–24 hours ⚬ Baking Time: 15 minutes

1 loaf French bread, cut in 1-inch-thick slices

1½ cups milk

4 eggs

½ cup orange juice

¼ cup sugar

1 Tbsp. vanilla extract, *optional*

Cinnamon, *optional*

Confectioners' sugar, *optional*

1. Arrange the bread slices in a 9×13-inch baking pan.

2. In a mixing bowl, beat the milk, eggs, orange juice, sugar, and vanilla together until well blended.

3. Pour over the bread.

4. Cover and refrigerate for 1 to 24 hours, according to your schedule.

5. Transfer the bread to a greased 10×15-inch pan, making sure slices don't touch. Dust with cinnamon, if you wish.

6. Bake 15 minutes at 400°F, or until puffy and lightly browned.

7. Dust with confectioners' sugar, if using, just before serving.

French Toast Casserole

CHILLED OVEN

Stacy Stoltzfus, Grantham, PA
Kaye Taylor, Florissant, MO

Makes 12 servings

Prep. Time: 10–15 minutes ❧ Chilling Time: Overnight ❧ Cooking/Baking Time: 45 minutes

10 slices bread, cubed
2 (8-oz.) pkgs. cream cheese
12 eggs, beaten well
2 cups milk
Cinnamon, *optional*

1. Place half of the bread cubes in a greased 9×13-inch pan.

2. Cube the cream cheese and scatter on top of the bread.

3. Put the rest of the bread cubes on top.

4. In a large bowl, use an electric mixer to beat the eggs and milk. Pour the mixture over the top of the bread and cream cheese.

5. Sprinkle the top with cinnamon, if you wish.

6. Refrigerate overnight. In the morning, bake at 375°F for 45 minutes. Cut into squares or dish out with a spoon.

Serving suggestion:

Serve hot with syrup. (Fruit syrups are especially good.)

Tip:

You can add fruit scattered with the cream cheese cubes: berries, diced apples, peaches, etc.

Jam Pockets

Jennifer Archer, Kalona, IA

Makes 4 servings

Prep. Time: 15 minutes   *Cooking/Baking Time: 18–20 minutes*

8-count tube refrigerated crescent rolls

Flour for work surface

4 Tbsp. cream cheese

4 Tbsp. fruit jam, flavor of your choice

1. Carefully unroll the rolls on lightly floured surface. Divide along dots to form 4 equal rectangles.

2. Gently pinch and smooth the dough to eliminate the diagonal dotted lines.

3. Place 1 tablespoon of cream cheese and 1 tablespoon of jam in the center of each rectangle. Bring the corners to the center and pinch together to seal.

4. Transfer to a baking sheet and bake at 400°F for 18 to 20 minutes.

Tip:

Double the pleasure by placing 1 tablespoon of cream cheese and 1 tablespoon of jam on each single triangle (rather than on each rectangle, formed by 2 triangles). Or place 2 tablespoons of cream cheese and 2 tablespoons of jam on each rectangle.

Streusel Cake

Jean Butzer, Batavia, NY

SLOW COOKER

Makes 8–10 servings

Prep. Time: 10 minutes   Cooking Time: 3–4 hours   Ideal slow-cooker size: 3-qt.

16-oz. pkg. pound cake mix, prepared according to package directions

¼ cup packed brown sugar

1 Tbsp. flour

¼ cup chopped nuts

1 tsp. cinnamon

1. Liberally grease and flour a 2-lb. metal coffee can, or slow-cooker baking insert, that fits into your slow cooker. Pour the prepared cake mix into the coffee can or baking insert.

2. In a small bowl, mix the brown sugar, flour, nuts, and cinnamon together. Sprinkle over the top of the cake mix.

3. Place the coffee can or baking insert into the slow cooker. Cover the top of tin or insert with several layers of paper towels.

4. Cover cooker itself and cook on High for 3 to 4 hours, or until a toothpick inserted in the center of the cake comes out clean.

5. Remove the baking tin from the slow cooker and allow to cool for 30 minutes before cutting into wedges to serve.

Old-Fashioned Crumb Cake

Mary Jane Musser, Manheim, PA
Sharon L. Anders, Alburtis, PA

Makes 12 servings

Prep. Time: 5–10 minutes & *Baking Time: 35–40 minutes*

3 cups flour

2 cups sugar

½ cup shortening

I tsp. baking soda

I cup milk

1. In a large mixing bowl, mix the flour and sugar together.

2. Cut the shortening into the flour-sugar mixture with a pastry cutter until crumbly.

3. Reserve 1 cup of crumbs for topping. Set aside.

4. In a small bowl, dissolve the baking soda in the milk. Stir into the dry mixture until thoroughly mixed.

5. Put the batter into two greased 8-inch pans. Top with the reserved crumbs.

6. Bake at 350°F for 35 minutes, or until a tester inserted in the center of the pans comes out clean.

Tip:

To add flavor, add ½ tsp. cinnamon to Step 1.

Breakfast Bread Pudding

Jean H. Robinson, Cinnaminson, NJ

Makes 6–8 servings

Prep. Time: 10 minutes ⚜ *Standing Time: 20 minutes–8 hours* ⚜ *Baking Time: 1 hour*

Nonstick cooking spray

½ loaf French bread, cut into 16 1-inch-thick slices

6 large eggs

2½ cups milk or half-and-half

½ cup honey

2 Tbsp. orange zest

Maple syrup, *optional*

1. Spray a 9×12-inch baking pan with nonstick cooking spray.

2. In the baking pan, lay the bread slices flat.

3. In a large mixing bowl, beat together the eggs, milk, honey, and orange zest. Pour over the bread slices and allow bread to absorb liquid for 20 minutes, or overnight if that's more convenient for you. (Cover the bread and refrigerate it if it will be standing overnight.)

4. Bake for 60 minutes at 350°F.

5. Allow to stand for 10 minutes before serving. Serve with maple syrup as a topping, if using.

Apple Cinnamon Pan Biscuits

Gretchen Maust, Keezletown, VA

Makes 20 servings

Prep. Time: 10 minutes ⚓ Cooking Time: 15–20 minutes

3½ cups self-rising flour
½ tsp. cinnamon
⅔ cup shortening
1 large apple
1¼ cups milk

1. In a mixing bowl, stir the flour and cinnamon to combine. Cut in the shortening with a pastry cutter until thoroughly mixed.

2. Grate the apple and stir it gently into mixture.

3. Add the milk and mix lightly. Too much stirring will cause the biscuits to be tough.

4. Pat the dough into a greased jelly-roll pan. Bake at 400°F just until lightly browned.

5. Add Topping (recipe below) if you wish. Cut into squares and serve warm.

Optional Topping:

When the biscuits finish baking, drizzle with a glaze made by mixing 2 Tbsp. melted butter, 3 Tbsp. milk, 1½ cups confectioners' sugar, and ½ tsp. cinnamon together or sprinkle with confectioners' sugar.

Blueberry Fancy

Leticia A. Zehr, Lowville, NY

Makes 12 servings

Prep. Time: 10–15 minutes ❧ *Cooking Time: 3–4 hours* ❧ *Ideal slow-cooker size: 5-qt.*

1 loaf Italian bread, cubed, *divided*
1 pt. blueberries, *divided*
8 oz. cream cheese, cubed, *divided*
6 eggs
1 ½ cups milk

1. Place half the bread cubes in the slow cooker.

2. Drop half the blueberries over top the bread.

3. Sprinkle half the cream cheese cubes over the blueberries.

4. Repeat all 3 layers.

5. In a mixing bowl, whisk together the eggs and milk. Pour over all ingredients in the slow cooker.

6. Cover and cook on Low until the dish is custardy and set.

7. Serve with maple syrup or blueberry sauce.

Variation:

Add 1 tsp. vanilla to Step 5.

Breakfast Sausage Ring

Joanne E. Martin, Stevens, PA

Makes 8 servings

Prep. Time: 15 minutes   ♣   *Cooking Time: 40–45 minutes*   ♣   *Standing Time: 10 minutes*

2 lb. bulk pork sausage
2 eggs, beaten
1½ cups fine dry bread crumbs
¼ cup chopped parsley, *optional*
Salt to taste, *optional*
Pepper to taste, *optional*

1. Lightly grease a 9-inch oven-safe ring mold.

2. In a large mixing bowl, mix all ingredients well. Then pack into the mold.

3. Bake at 350°F for 20 minutes.

4. Remove from the oven and pour off any accumulated fat. Return to oven to bake for 20 minutes more.

5. Remove from the oven and allow to stand for 10 minutes. Turn onto a platter and fill the center with scrambled eggs.

Breakfast Sausage Casserole

Kendra Dreps, Liberty, PA

Makes 8 servings

Prep. Time: 15 minutes ⚜ *Chilling Time: 8 hours* ⚜ *Cooking Time: 4 hours* ⚜ *Ideal slow-cooker size: 3-qt.*

1 lb. loose turkey sausage

6 eggs

2 cups unsweetened almond milk

8 slices whole-grain or sprouted-grain bread, cubed

2 cups reduced-fat shredded cheddar cheese

1. In a nonstick skillet, brown and drain the sausage.

2. Mix together the eggs and milk in a large bowl.

3. Stir in the bread cubes, cheese, and sausage.

4. Place in a greased slow cooker.

5. Refrigerate overnight.

6. Cook on Low 4 hours.

Variation:

Use cubed cooked ham instead of sausage.

Easy Egg and Sausage Puff

Sara Kinsinger, Stuarts Draft, VA

Makes 6 servings

Prep. Time: 10–15 minutes ⚬ *Cooking Time: 2–2½ hours* ⚬ *Ideal slow-cooker size: 2- to 4-qt.*

I lb. bulk sausage
6 eggs
I cup all-purpose baking mix
I cup shredded cheddar cheese
2 cups milk
¼ tsp. dry mustard, *optional*

1. Brown the sausage in nonstick skillet. Break up chunks of the meat as it cooks. Drain.

2. Meanwhile, spray the interior of a slow cooker with nonstick cooking spray.

3. Mix all the ingredients in the slow cooker.

4. Cover and cook on High 1 hour. Turn to Low and cook for 1 to 1½ hours, or until the dish is fully cooked in the center.

Mom's Heavenly Quiche

Barbara Forrester Landis, Lititz, PA

Makes 6–8 servings

Prep. Time: 15 minutes ⚘ *Baking Time: 40–50 minutes*

6 eggs, or equivalent amount of egg substitute

2 Tbsp. flour

2 cups cottage cheese

1 cup shredded cheddar cheese

½ stick (4 Tbsp.) butter, melted

4-oz. can diced green chilies, undrained, *optional*

1. In a good-sized mixing bowl, beat the eggs or pour in egg substitute.

2. Stir in the flour.

3. When well mixed, stir in the cottage cheese, shredded cheese, and butter, and the diced green chilies, if using.

4. Pour into a greased 10-inch pie plate.

5. Bake for 40 to 45 minutes, or until set in center. Insert the blade of a knife in the center. If it comes out clean, the quiche is finished. If it doesn't, bake for 5 more minutes. Test again, and continue baking if needed.

6. Let stand 10 minutes before cutting to allow cheeses to firm up.

Tips:

1. You can use any kind of flour. I use whole wheat.

2. You can use any kind of cottage cheese. I use low-fat.

3. This is delicious eaten cold the next day if there's any left.

4. If you have leftover cooked veggies in your refrigerator, place them in the bottom of the pan and cover with egg mixture as a variation.

Breakfast Pizza

Jessica Hont, Coatesville, PA

Makes 8 servings

Prep. Time: 10 minutes & Baking Time: 20–35 minutes

10-oz. refrigerated pizza crust

8 eggs

¼ cup milk or cream

6 slices bacon, cooked crisp and crumbled

2 cups shredded cheddar or Monterey Jack cheese

1. Unroll the pizza crust onto a baking sheet.

2. Bake at 425°F for 10 minutes.

3. In a large mixing bowl, whisk together the eggs and milk.

4. In a skillet, cook the mixture until the eggs start to congeal, about 3–4 minutes. Spoon onto the crust.

5. Top with the bacon and cheese.

6. Bake for an additional 10 minutes until eggs are set and crust is golden brown.

Breakfast Casserole

Jean Butzer, Batavia, NY

Makes 4–6 servings

Prep. Time: 20 minutes   Cooking Time: 1 hour

1 lb. bulk sausage

30-oz. pkg. frozen shredded hash browns, thawed

16-oz. container French onion dip

2 cups sour cream

2 cups shredded cheddar cheese, *divided*

1. In a skillet, brown the sausage. Drain.

2. In a large mixing bowl, combine the browned sausage, hash browns, French onion dip, sour cream, and 1 cup shredded cheese.

3. Spread the mixture in a greased 9×13-inch baking pan. Bake at 350°F for 45 minutes.

4. Sprinkle with the remaining cheese and bake for an additional 15 minutes.

Breakfast Pie

Darlene Bloom, San Antonio, TX

Makes 6 servings

Prep. Time: 20 minutes & Baking Time: 30 minutes & Standing Time: 5–10 minutes

8 oz. lower-sodium ham

1 cup chopped bell pepper, red or green, *optional*

1 ½ tsp. dried minced onions

1 cup 75%-less-fat shredded cheddar cheese

½ cup reduced-fat buttermilk baking mix

1 cup nonfat milk

2 eggs

1. In a skillet, brown the meat and the bell pepper, if using, with the dried minced onions. Drain off the drippings.

2. Place the cooked ingredients in a greased 9-inch pie plate.

3. Top with a layer of shredded cheese.

4. In a mixing bowl, whisk baking mix, milk, and eggs together. Pour over the ingredients in the pie plate.

5. Bake at 400°F for 30 minutes.

6. Allow to stand for 5 to 10 minutes before cutting and serving.

Tips:

1. Double this recipe and prepare in a 9x13-inch baking pan. I take this to potlucks all the time (warm) out of the oven.

2. You can use ground turkey or beef as your choice of meats and add 1 envelope taco seasoning mix to the skillet as you cook. I call this version Taco Bake and often make it for dinner.

3. You can replace the dried minced onion with a small, diced onion instead if you have time.

Potato-Bacon Gratin

Valerie Drobel, Carlisle, PA

Makes 6 servings

Prep. Time: 15 minutes   Baking Time: 1 hour

6-oz. bag fresh spinach

1½ tsp. garlic powder

1 Tbsp. olive oil

4 large potatoes, peeled or unpeeled, *divided*

6 oz. Canadian bacon slices, *divided*

6 oz. grated Swiss, cheddar, or Gruyère cheese, *divided*

1 cup chicken broth

1. In a large skillet, sauté the spinach and garlic powder in olive oil just until spinach is wilted.

2. Cut the potatoes into thin slices.

3. In a 2-qt. baking dish, layer ⅓ of the potatoes, half of the bacon, ⅓ of the cheese, and half of the wilted spinach.

4. Repeat the layers ending with potatoes. Reserve ⅓ of the cheese for later.

5. Pour the chicken broth over all.

6. Cover and bake at 350°F for 45 minutes.

7. Uncover and bake for 15 more minutes. During the last 5 minutes, top with remaining cheese.

8. Allow to stand for 10 minutes before serving.

Tip:

You can trade the garlic powder for 1 fresh minced clove of garlic instead.

Cheddar-Ham Oven Omelet

Jolene Schrock, Millersburg, OH

Makes 9–12 servings

Prep. Time: 10 minutes ⚬ *Cooking/Baking Time: 40–45 minutes* ⚬ *Standing Time: 10 minutes*

16 eggs

2 cups milk

8 oz. shredded cheddar cheese

¾ cup cubed fully cooked ham

6 scallions

Chopped sliced mushrooms, *optional*

Chopped green peppers, *optional*

1. In a large bowl, beat the eggs and milk until well blended. Stir in the cheese, ham, and onions. Add the scallions and the mushrooms and green peppers, if using.

2. Pour the egg mixture into a greased 9×13-inch baking dish.

3. Bake, uncovered, at 350°F for 40 to 45 minutes, or until a knife inserted near the center comes out clean. Let stand 10 minutes before cutting and serving.

Variation:

Add ½ tsp. salt and ¼ tsp. pepper, if you wish, to Step 1.

Huevos Rancheros

Pat Bishop, Bedminster, PA

Makes 6 servings

Prep. Time: 25 minutes ⚜ *Cooking Time: 2 hours* ⚜ *Ideal slow-cooker size: 6-qt.*

3 cups gluten-free salsa, room temperature

2 cups cooked beans, drained, room temperature

6 eggs, room temperature

Salt to taste

Pepper to taste

⅓ cup reduced-fat grated Mexican-blend cheese, *optional*

1. In a slow cooker, mix the salsa and beans.

2. Cook on High for 1 hour or until steaming.

3. With a spoon, make 6 evenly spaced dents in the salsa mixture; try not to expose the bottom of the crock. Break an egg into each dent.

4. Salt and pepper the eggs. Sprinkle with the cheese, if using.

5. Cover and continue to cook on High until the egg whites are set and the yolks are as firm as you like them, approximately 20–40 minutes.

6. To serve, scoop out an egg with some beans and salsa.

Serving Suggestion:

Serve with warm white corn tortillas.

Slow-Cooker Oatmeal

Martha Bender, New Paris, IN

Makes 7–8 servings

Prep. Time: 10–15 minutes ⚬ *Cooking Time: 8–9 hours* ⚬ *Ideal slow-cooker size: 4- to 5-qt.*

2 cups gluten-free rolled oats

4 cups water

I large apple, peeled and chopped

I cup raisins

I tsp. cinnamon

I–2 Tbsp. orange zest

1. In a slow cooker, combine all the ingredients.

2. Cover and cook on Low for 8 to 9 hours.

Serving suggestion:

Serve topped with brown sugar, if you wish, and milk.

Oatmeal Morning

Barbara Forrester Landis, Lititz, PA

Makes 6 servings

Prep. Time: 5 minutes ❧ Cooking Time: 4 minutes ❧ Setting: Manual
Pressure: High ❧ Release: Natural

1 cup water
2 cups uncooked steel cut oats
1 cup dried cranberries
1 cup walnuts
½ teaspoon salt
1 tablespoon cinnamon
1 cup water
2 cups nonfat milk

1. Place the steaming rack into the inner pot of an Instant Pot and pour in the water.

2. In an approximately 7-cup heat-safe baking dish, add all of the remaining ingredients and stir.

3. Place the dish on top of the steaming rack, close the lid, and secure it to a locking position.

4. Be sure the vent is set to sealing, then set the Instant Pot for 4 minutes on Manual.

5. When it is done cooking, allow the pressure to release naturally.

6. Carefully remove the rack and dish from the Instant Pot and serve.

Poached Eggs

Hope Comerford, Clinton Township, MI

Makes 6–8 servings

Prep. Time: 5 minutes ⚶ *Cooking Time: 2–5 minutes* ⚶ *Setting: Steam*
Pressure: High ⚶ *Release: Manual*

I cup water
Nonstick cooking spray
4 large eggs

1. Place the trivet in the bottom of the inner pot of an Instant Pot and pour in the water.

2. You will need small silicone egg poacher cups that will fit in your Instant Pot to hold the eggs. Spray each silicone cup with nonstick cooking spray.

3. Crack each egg and pour it into the prepared cup.

4. Very carefully place the silicone cups into the Inner Pot so they do not spill.

5. Secure the lid by locking it into place and turn the vent to the sealing position.

6. Push the Steam button and adjust the time—2 minutes for a very runny egg all the way to 5 minutes for a slightly runny egg.

7. When the timer beeps, release the pressure manually and remove the lid, being very careful not to let the condensation in the lid drip into your eggs.

8. Very carefully remove the silicone cups from the inner pot.

9. Carefully remove the poached eggs from each silicone cup and serve immediately.

SOUPS, STEWS & CHILIES

MEATLESS

Butternut Squash Soup

Colleen Heatwole, Burton, MI

Makes: 4 servings

Prep. Time: 30 minutes   ⚬   Cooking Time: 15 minutes   ⚬   Setting: Sauté and Manual
Pressure: High   ⚬   Release: Manual

2 Tbsp. butter

1 large onion, chopped

2 cloves garlic, minced

1 tsp. thyme

½ tsp. sage

Salt to taste

Pepper to taste

2 large butternut squash, peeled, seeded, and cubed (about 4 lb.)

4 cups vegetable stock

1. In the inner pot of the Instant Pot, melt the butter using the sauté function.

2. Add the onion and garlic and cook until soft, 3 to 5 minutes.

3. Add the thyme and sage and cook another minute. Season with salt and pepper.

4. Stir in the butternut squash and add the chicken stock.

5. Secure the lid and make sure vent is at sealing. Using Manual setting, cook squash and seasonings 10 minutes, using high pressure.

6. When time is up, do a quick release of the pressure.

7. Puree the soup in a food processor or use an immersion blender right in the inner pot. If the soup is too thick, add more stock. Adjust salt and pepper as needed.

Creamy Broccoli Soup

SuAnne Burkholder, Millersburg, OH

Makes 3–4 servings

Prep. Time: 10–15 minutes & *Cooking Time: 15–20 minutes*

4 cups milk, *divided*
1 Tbsp. vegetable stock
1½ cups chopped broccoli
1 Tbsp. water
2 Tbsp. cornstarch
Salt to taste

1. In a stockpot over low heat, heat 3 cups of milk and the chicken stock until hot.

2. Meanwhile, place the broccoli in a microwave-safe dish. Add 1 Tbsp. water. Cover. Microwave on High for 1½ minutes. Stir. Repeat until the broccoli becomes bright green and just tender. Be careful not to overcook it! Drain the liquid from the broccoli.

3. In a small bowl, or in a jar with a tight-fitting lid, mix together 1 cup milk and the cornstarch until smooth. Slowly add to hot milk mixture.

4. Simmer gently, stirring constantly. When slightly thickened, add the broccoli and salt.

Creamy Tomato Soup

Sara Kinsinger, Stuarts Draft, VA

Makes 6 servings

Prep. Time: 20 minutes ⚘ *Cooking Time: 1½ hours* ⚘ *Ideal slow-cooker size: 4-qt.*

26-oz. can condensed tomato soup, plus 6 oz. water to equal 1 qt.

½ tsp. salt, *optional*

½ stick (4 Tbsp.) butter

8 Tbsp. flour

1 qt. milk (whole or reduced-fat)

1. In a slow cooker, mix the tomato soup, salt (if using), and butter to combine.

2. Cover and cook on High for 1 hour.

3. Meanwhile, place the flour and 1 cup of milk in a 2-qt. microwave-safe container. Whisk together until the big lumps disappear. Then whisk in the remaining milk until only small lumps remain.

4. Place flour-milk mixture in the microwave and cook on High for 3 minutes. Remove and stir until smooth. Return to the microwave and cook on High for another 3 minutes.

5. In the slow cooker, add the thickened milk slowly to the hot soup.

6. Heat thoroughly for 10 to 15 minutes.

Tip:

Serve with freshly ground pepper, dried chives, or your choice of green herbs, and oyster crackers or croutons.

Quickie French Onion Soup

Mary Puskar, Forest Hill, MD

Makes 6–8 servings

Prep. Time: 5–10 minutes   &   Cooking Time: 1 hour

½ stick (4 Tbsp.) butter

3–4 large onions (enough to make 5 cups sliced onions)

¼ cup flour

6 cups beef broth, or 3 14½-oz. cans beef broth, or 6 cups water with 6 beef bouillon cubes

6–8 melba rounds, *optional*

2 cups grated mozzarella cheese, *optional*

1. In a large saucepan, melt the butter.

2. Meanwhile, slice the onions.

3. Sauté the onions in the butter. After they become tender, continue cooking over low heat so that they brown and deepen in flavor, for up to 30 minutes.

4. Sprinkle with the flour. Cook for 2 minutes.

5. Stir in the broth. Cover.

6. Heat to boiling and simmer for 20 minutes.

7. Ladle into individual serving bowls.

8. Top each bowl with melba rounds and/or grated cheese if you wish. For extra beauty and flavor, broil until the cheese melts, but first make sure that the soup bowls can withstand the broiler heat. They could crack.

Tip:

This recipe doubles very easily.

Kale Chowder

Colleen Heatwole, Burton, MI

Makes 8 servings

Prep. Time: 30 minutes ⚘ *Cooking Time: 4 to 6 hours* ⚘ *Ideal slow-cooker size: 5-qt.*

8 cups chicken broth

1 bunch kale, cleaned, stems removed, coarsely chopped

2 lb. potatoes, peeled and diced

1 medium onion, diced

1 lb. cooked ham

1½ Tbsp. garlic powder

½ tsp. pepper, or to taste

1. In a slow cooker, combine all the ingredients.

2. Cover and cook on Low for 4 to 6 hours, until the vegetables are tender.

Variations:

1. Turkey ham can be used instead of regular ham.

2. Use 3 or 4 fresh cloves garlic instead of the garlic powder.

Italian Bean Soup

SLOW COOKER

Eylene Egan, Babylon, NY

Makes 8 servings

Prep. Time: 10 minutes ❧ *Cooking Time: 8–10 hours* ❧ *Ideal slow-cooker size: 4-qt.*

1 lb. dried baby lima beans

15 cups water, *divided*

2 8-oz. cans low-sodium tomato sauce

3–4 cloves garlic, minced

Salt to taste

Pepper to taste

1. In a large stockpot, cover the beans with 9 cups of water. Cover the pot and bring to a boil.

2. Boil for 10 minutes. Remove from the heat and allow the beans to stand for 1 hour, covered.

3. Return to the stove top, keep covered, and bring to a boil. Reduce heat to a simmer, and continue cooking for 2½ to 3 hours, or until the beans are tender. Drain.

4. Place drained, cooked beans in the slow cooker. Add the tomato sauce, the garlic, 6 cups of water, salt, and pepper, and stir together well.

5. Cover and cook on High for 1 hour, and then cook on Low for 4 to 5 hours.

Chipotle Navy Bean Soup

Rebecca Weybright, Manheim, PA

Makes 6 servings

Prep. Time: 10 minutes ⚶ Cooking Time: 8 hours
Standing Time: 12 hours ⚶ Ideal slow-cooker size: 5-qt.

1½ cups dried navy beans, soaked overnight

1 onion, chopped

1 dried chipotle chile, soaked 10–15 minutes in cold water

4 cups water

1–2 tsp. salt

2 cups canned reduced-sodium tomatoes with juice

1. Drain the soaked beans.

2. Add the beans to the slow cooker with the onion, chile, and 4 cups of water.

3. Cover and cook on Low for 8 hours until the beans are creamy.

4. Add the salt and tomatoes.

5. Use an immersion blender to puree the soup.

CHICKEN

Chicken Noodle Soup

STOVETOP

Colleen Heatwole, Burton, MI

Makes 8 servings

Prep. Time: 15 minutes ✂ *Cooking Time: 45–50 minutes*

2½ qts. chicken stock
½ cup diced celery
½ cup diced carrots
8-oz. pkg. egg noodles
2 cups cooked, diced chicken
Salt, *optional*

1. In a medium stockpot, bring the stock to a boil.

2. Add the celery and carrots. Simmer for about 7 minutes, or until the vegetables are tender but not overcooked.

3. Add the noodles and chicken. Return the soup to a boil. Continue to cook for another 5 to 7 minutes, or until the noodles are tender but not mushy.

4. Add salt, if using.

Chicken Rice Soup

Norma Grieser, Clarksville, MI

Makes 8 servings

Prep. Time: 30 minutes ☙ Cooking Time: 4–8 hours ☙ Ideal slow-cooker size: 4- to 6-qt.

4 cups chicken broth
4 cups chopped chicken, cooked
1⅓ cups chopped celery
1⅓ cups diced carrots
1 qt. water
1 cup uncooked long-grain rice

1. In a slow cooker, combine all the ingredients.

2. Cover and cook on Low for 4 to 8 hours, or until the vegetables are cooked to your liking.

Tip:

If you like your soup less thick, keep the long-grain rice out and cook it separately. When serving, spoon the rice into individual bowls with the soup ladled over the top.

Chunky Chicken Vegetable Soup

SLOW COOKER

Janice Muller, Derwood, MD

Makes 6 servings

Prep. Time: 20 minutes ❧ *Cooking Time: 2–6 hours* ❧ *Ideal slow-cooker size: 3½- to 4-qt.*

2½ cups water

8-oz. can tomato sauce

10-oz. pkg. frozen mixed vegetables, partially thawed

1½ tsp. Italian seasoning

1 envelope dry chicken noodle soup mix

2 cups chopped cooked chicken or turkey

1. In a slow cooker, combine all the ingredients.

2. Cook on Low for 2 to 6 hours, depending upon how crunchy you like your vegetables.

Quick Taco Chicken Soup

Karen Waggoner, Joplin, MO

Makes 4–6 servings

Prep. Time: 5 minutes ⚬ *Cooking Time: 1 hour* ⚬ *Ideal slow-cooker size: 4-qt.*

12-oz. can cooked chicken, undrained
14-oz. can chicken broth
16-oz. jar mild thick-and-chunky salsa
15-oz. can ranch-style beans
15-oz. can whole-kernel corn

1. In a slow cooker, combine all the ingredients.

2. Cover and cook on High for 1 hour. Keep warm on Low until ready to serve.

PORK

Potato Cheese Soup

Mary Kathryn Yoder, Harrisonville, MO

Makes 5 servings

Prep. Time: 20 minutes   ⚓   Cooking Time: 20 minutes

4 medium potatoes, peeled and cut into chunks

4 bacon slices

1 small onion, chopped, *optional*

4 cups milk

¾ tsp. salt

Pepper to taste

¾ cup shredded cheese, your choice of flavors

1. Place the potato chunks in a saucepan. Add 1 inch water. Cover and cook over low heat until very tender.

2. Meanwhile, cut the bacon into 1-inch lengths. Place the bacon in a large saucepan, along with the onion, if using. Cook until tender.

3. When the potatoes become tender, mash in their cooking water.

4. Add the mashed potatoes and milk to the bacon, and to the onion, if using.

5. Stir in salt, pepper, and the cheese. Cook over low heat, stirring occasionally to distribute cheese as it melts.

6. Soup is ready when the cheese is melted and the soup is hot.

Broccoli Rabe and Sausage Soup

Carlene Horne, Bedford, NH

Makes 4 servings

Prep. Time: 15 minutes   Cooking Time: 15 minutes

2 Tbsp. olive oil

1 onion, chopped

1 lb. sweet or spicy sausage, casing removed, sliced

1 bunch broccoli rabe, approximately 5 cups chopped

32 oz. chicken broth

1 cup water

8 oz. frozen tortellini

1. In a stockpot, heat the olive oil.

2. Add the onion and sausage and sauté until tender.

3. Add the broccoli rabe and sauté for a few more minutes.

4. Pour the broth and water into the stockpot pan; bring to a simmer.

5. Add the tortellini and cook a few minutes until tender.

Tip:

Substitute any green, such as Swiss chard, kale, or spinach, for the broccoli rabe.

Serving suggestion:

Serve with grated cheese and crusty bread.

Pork Potato Soup

Kristin Tice, Shipshewana, IN

Makes 4 servings

Prep. Time: 20 minutes ❧ Cooking Time: 4 hours ❧ Ideal slow-cooker size: 3-qt.

1 lb. ground pork

½ cup chopped onion

1 sweet potato, cubed and peeled, approximately 3 cups

2 beef bouillon cubes

½ tsp. dried rosemary

3 cups water

1. In a nonstick skillet, brown the meat and the onion.

2. Place the drained meat, along with the onion, into slow cooker. Add the remaining ingredients.

3. Cover and cook on Low for 4 hours.

Variation:

Add a bit of hot sauce to make the soup spicy, or serve on the side to accommodate those who don't like hot food.

Hearty Lentil and Sausage Stew

Cindy Krestynick, Glen Lyon, PA

Makes 6 servings

Prep. Time: 5–10 minutes ☙ Cooking Time: 4–6 hours ☙ Ideal slow-cooker size: 6-qt.

2 cups dry lentils, picked over and rinsed

14½-oz. can diced tomatoes

8 cups canned chicken broth, or water

1 Tbsp. salt

½–1 lb. pork or beef sausage, cut into 2-inch pieces

1. In a slow cooker, stir the lentils, tomatoes, chicken broth, and salt to combine. Place the sausage pieces on top.

2. Cover and cook on Low for 4 to 6 hours, or until the lentils are tender but not dry or mushy.

Old-Fashioned Bean Soup

Shirley Sears, Sarasota, FL

Makes 8–10 servings

Prep. Time: 10 minutes ⚬ Cooking Time: 13–20 hours ⚬ Ideal slow-cooker size: 4- to 5-qt.

1 lb. dried navy beans, soaked overnight

16 cups water, *divided*

1 lb. meaty ham bones, or ham pieces

1 tsp. salt

½ tsp. pepper

½ cup chopped celery leaves

1 medium onion, chopped

1 bay leaf, *optional*

1. Place the dried beans and 8 cups of water in a large stockpot. Cover and allow to soak for 8 hours or overnight. Drain.

2. In a slow cooker, combine the soaked beans and 8 cups of fresh water.

3. Add all the remaining ingredients.

4. Cover and cook on Low for 10 to 12 hours, or on High for 5 to 6 hours, or until the meat is falling off the bone and the beans are tender but not mushy.

Bean and Bacon Soup

Jeanette Oberholtzer, Manheim, PA

Makes 6 servings

Prep. Time: 25 minutes ❧ *Cooking Time: 11–13½ hours* ❧ *Ideal slow-cooker size: 4-qt.*

1¼ cups dried bean soup mix, or any combination of mixed dried beans

8 cups water, *divided*

1 onion, chopped

4 slices fried bacon (precooked bacon works well), crumbled

1 envelope taco seasoning

2 14-oz. cans diced tomatoes, undrained

1. In a large stockpot, cover the dried beans with the water. Cover the pot and bring to a boil. Cook for 2 minutes over high heat.

2. Remove the pot from the heat and allow to stand, covered, for 1 hour. Return the pot to the stove top and cook covered for 2½ to 3 hours, or until the beans are tender. Drain.

3. In a slow cooker, combine the cooked beans, onion, 3 cups water, bacon, and taco seasoning. Mix well.

4. Cook on Low for 8 to 10 hours.

5. Add the tomatoes. Stir well. Cook for another 30 minutes.

Tip:
If you like a thickened soup, mash some of the beans before adding the tomatoes.

Split Pea Soup with Ham

Elena Yoder, Carlsbad, NM

Makes 8 servings

Prep. Time: 15 minutes ⚜ *Cooking Time: 4 hours* ⚜ *Ideal slow-cooker size: 4-qt.*

2½ qts. water

1 ham hock or pieces of chopped ham

2½ cups split peas, dried

1 medium onion, chopped

3 medium carrots, cut in small pieces

Salt to taste

Pepper to taste

1. In a saucepan over high heat, bring the water to a boil.

2. Place all other ingredients into slow cooker. In a slow cooker, combine the boiling water and all the other ingredients.

3. Cover and cook on High for 4 hours, or until the vegetables are tender.

4. If you've cooked a ham hock, remove it from the soup and debone the meat. Stir the chunks of meat back into the soup before serving.

Black Bean Soup

Dorothy VanDeest, Memphis, TN

Makes 8 servings

Prep. Time: 10 minutes to precook beans ⚬ *Cooking Time: 6½–8½ hours* ⚬ *Ideal slow-cooker size: 4-qt.*

1 lb. dried black beans

12 cups water, *divided*

¼ lb. bacon, fried crisp and crumbled,
or ½ lb. smoked ham, chopped

2 medium onions, chopped

1 tsp. garlic salt

¼ tsp. coarsely ground pepper

1. In a large stockpot, cover the dried beans with 9 cups water. Cover the pot and bring to a boil.

2. Boil for 10 minutes. Reduce the heat and simmer, covered, for 1½ hours, or until the beans are tender. Discard the cooking water.

3. In a slow cooker, combine the cooked beans, 3 cups water, bacon, onions, garlic salt, and pepper, stirring well.

4. Cover and cook on High for 4 to 6 hours.

Tip:

To serve beans as a side dish, add a 4-oz. can of chopped green chilies, 1 tsp. powdered cumin, and 1/4 tsp. dried oregano to 5–6 cups of fully cooked beans. Simmer for 25 minutes to blend flavors.

Beef Vegetable Soup

Margaret Moffitt, Bartlett, TN

Makes 12 servings

Prep. Time: 15 minutes & *Cooking Time: 6–8 hours* & *Ideal slow-cooker size: 4-qt.*

1 lb. chunks of stewing beef
28-oz. can stewed tomatoes, undrained
1 tomato can water
16-oz. pkg. of your favorite frozen vegetable
½ 10-oz. pkg. frozen chopped onions
1½ tsp. salt and ¼–½ tsp. pepper
2 Tbsp. chopped fresh parsley, *optional*

1. In a slow cooker, combine all the ingredients.

2. Cover and cook on High for 6 to 8 hours.

Italian Pasta Soup

Sharon Timpe, Jackson, WI

Makes 6 servings

Prep. Time: 10–15 minutes   Cooking Time: 30 minutes

2 (14½-oz.) cans chicken broth

1 cup water

1 cup uncooked elbow macaroni

18 frozen Italian-style or regular meatballs

2 cups fresh spinach leaves, finely shredded

8-oz. can pizza sauce

1. In a large stockpot, bring the broth and the water to a boil.

2. Add the pasta and meatballs and return to a boil. Lower the heat and continue cooking for 8 to 10 minutes, or until the pasta is done and the meatballs are hot. Stir occasionally. Do not drain.

3. Add the spinach and pizza sauce. Simmer for 2 minutes, or until heated thoroughly.

Hearty Beef Barley Soup

STOVETOP

Karen Gingrich, New Holland, PA

Makes 4–5 servings

Prep. Time: 5–10 minutes ⚹ *Cooking Time: 35 minutes*

1 lb. beef tips
2 cups sliced fresh mushrooms
¼ tsp. garlic powder
32-oz. can (3½ cups) beef broth
2 medium carrots, sliced
¼ tsp. dried thyme
Dash pepper
½ cup quick-cooking barley

1. In a nonstick saucepan, cook the beef until it is browned and the juices evaporate, about 10 minutes, stirring often.

2. Add the mushrooms and garlic powder and cook until the mushrooms begin to wilt, about 5 minutes.

3. Add the broth, carrots, thyme, and pepper.

4. Heat to a boil. Stir in the barley. Cover and cook over low heat for 20 minutes, or until the barley is tender.

Mediterranean Beef Stew

SLOW COOKER

Sandy Osborn, Iowa City, IA

Makes 4 servings

Prep. Time: 5–10 minutes ♣ Cooking Time: 3–8 hours ♣ Ideal slow-cooker size: 3½-qt.

2 medium zucchini, cut into bite-sized pieces

¾ lb. beef stew meat, cut into ½-inch pieces

2 (14½-oz.) cans Italian-style diced tomatoes, undrained

½ tsp. pepper, *optional*

2-inch stick cinnamon, or ¼ tsp. ground cinnamon

1. Place the zucchini in the bottom of a slow cooker.

2. Add the beef and remaining ingredients in the order they are listed.

3. Cover and cook on High for 3 to 5 hours, or until the meat is tender but not overcooked. You can also cook the stew on High for 1 hour, then on Low for 7 hours, or until the meat is tender but not overdone. Remove the cinnamon stick before serving.

Succulent Beef Stew

Linda Thomas, Sayner, WI

Makes 6 servings

Prep. Time: 30 minutes ⚬ Cooking Time: 8 hours ⚬ Ideal slow-cooker size: 3-qt.

1–1½ lb. stew meat

1 medium to large onion, chopped

Salt, *optional*

Pepper, *optional*

1¾ cups low-sodium beef broth

1 broth can water

5 shakes Worcestershire sauce, *optional*

2 bay leaves, *optional*

½ lb. baby carrots

5 medium white potatoes, peeled or unpeeled, cut into ½-inch chunks

1. In a nonstick skillet, brown the stew meat and onion. Sprinkle with salt and pepper, if using. Transfer the mixture to a slow cooker.

2. Add the broth and water. Add the Worcestershire sauce and bay leaves, if using. Stir together well.

3. Cover and cook on Low 4 hours.

4. Layer in the carrots and potatoes. Push down into liquid as much as you can. Cover and continue cooking on Low for 4 more hours.

5. If the stew seems to get dry, add ½ cup water.

Taco Soup

Norma Grieser, Clarksville, MI

Makes 4–6 servings

Prep. Time: 10–12 minutes   *Cooking Time: 4–6 hours*   *Ideal slow-cooker size: 3-qt.*

1 lb. ground beef
1 qt. tomato juice
15-oz. can kidney beans
1 envelope dry taco seasoning
10½-oz. can tomato soup
Medium onion, chopped, *optional*

1. In a nonstick skillet, brown the beef. Drain. Place in a slow cooker.

2. Add the remaining ingredients to the slow cooker and stir until well combined.

3. Cover and cook on Low for 4 to 6 hours.

Tip:

Serve with Doritos, sour cream, and shredded cheddar cheese as toppings, if you wish.

Variation:

Instead of tomato juice and tomato soup, substitute 1 14½-oz. can stewed tomatoes and 1 8-oz. can tomato sauce.

—Sharon Shank, Bridgewater, VA

Chunky Beef Chili

Ruth C. Hancock, Earlsboro, OK

Makes 4 servings

Prep. Time: 30 minutes & Cooking Time: 1¾–2¼ hours

2 Tbsp. vegetable oil, *divided*

1 lb. stew beef, cut into 1½-inch thick pieces

1 medium onion, chopped

1 medium jalapeño pepper with seeds, minced, *optional*

½ tsp. salt

2 (14½-oz.) cans chili-seasoned diced tomatoes

1. In a stockpot over medium heat, heat 1 Tbsp. oil until hot.

2. Brown half of the beef in the oil. Remove the meat from the pot and keep it warm.

3. Repeat with the remaining beef. Remove the meat from the pot and keep it warm.

4. Add the remaining 1 Tbsp. oil to stockpot, along with the onion and the pepper, if using.

5. Cook for 5 to 8 minutes, or until the vegetables are tender. Stir occasionally.

6. Return the meat and juices to the stockpot. Add the salt and tomatoes.

7. Bring to a boil. Reduce the heat. Cover tightly and simmer for 1¾ to 2¼ hours, or until the meat is tender but not dried out.

Quick and Easy Chili

Carolyn Spohn, Shawnee, KS

Makes 3–4 servings

Prep. Time: 10 minutes   Cooking Time: 25 minutes

½ lb. ground beef, or turkey, browned and drained

1 medium onion, chopped

2 cloves garlic, minced

2 (15-oz.) cans chili-style beans with liquid

8-oz. can tomato sauce

1. In a large skillet, brown the ground beef.

2. Drain, leaving about 1 tsp. drippings in pan. Sauté the onion and garlic until softened.

3. Add the beans, with liquid, and the tomato sauce. Bring to a slow boil.

4. Reduce the heat to a simmer and cook for 15 minutes.

5. Return the meat to the skillet. Heat together for 5 minutes.

MAIN DISHES

MEATLESS

Stuffed Pasta Shells

Jean M. Butzer, Batavia, NY
Lori Lehman, Ephrata, PA
Rhoda Atzeff, Lancaster, PA

Makes 12–14 servings

Prep. Time: 30–45 minutes ⚮ *Cooking/Baking Time: 30–45 minutes*

1 lb. shredded mozzarella cheese

15-oz. container ricotta cheese

10-oz. pkg. frozen chopped spinach, thawed and squeezed dry

12-oz. pkg. jumbo pasta shells, cooked and drained

28-oz. jar spaghetti sauce

1. In a large mixing bowl, combine the cheeses and spinach.

2. Stuff a rounded tablespoonful of the cheese and spinach mixture into each shell.

3. Arrange the filled shells in a greased 9×13-inch baking dish.

4. Pour the spaghetti sauce over the shells.

5. Cover and bake at 350°F for 30 to 45 minutes, or until heated through.

Baked Ziti

Hope Comerford, Clinton Township, MI

Makes 8 servings

Prep. Time: 15 minutes   ⚹   Cooking Time: 4 hours   ⚹   Ideal slow-cooker size: 5-qt.

Nonstick cooking spray

1 (28-oz.) can low-sodium crushed tomatoes

1 (15-oz.) can low-sodium tomato sauce

1½ tsp. Italian seasoning

1 tsp. garlic powder

1 tsp. onion powder

1 tsp. pepper

1 tsp. sea salt

1 lb. ziti or rigatoni pasta, uncooked, *divided*

1–2 cups low-fat shredded mozzarella cheese, *divided*

1. Spray a slow-cooker crock with nonstick cooking spray.

2. In a bowl, mix together the crushed tomatoes, tomato sauce, Italian seasoning, garlic powder, onion powder, pepper, and salt.

3. In the bottom of the crock, pour ⅓ of the pasta sauce.

4. Add ½ of the pasta on top of the sauce.

5. Add another ⅓ of the pasta sauce.

6. Spread ½ of the mozzarella cheese on top of that.

7. Add the remaining pasta, the remaining sauce, and the remaining cheese on top of that.

8. Cover and cook on Low for 4 hours.

Eggplant Italian

Melanie Thrower, McPherson, KS

Makes 6–8 servings

Prep. Time: 30 minutes ⚘ *Cooking Time: 4 hours* ⚘ *Ideal slow-cooker size: 4- or 5-qt. oval*

2 eggplants

Nonstick cooking spray

¼ cup Egg Beaters

24 oz. fat-free cottage cheese

¼ tsp. salt

Black pepper to taste

14-oz. can tomato sauce

2–4 Tbsp. Italian seasoning, according to your taste preference

1. Peel the eggplants and cut them into ½-inch-thick slices. Soak in salt water for about 5 minutes to remove bitterness. Drain well.

2. Spray the slow cooker with nonstick cooking spray.

3. In a bowl, mix the Egg Beaters, cottage cheese, salt, and pepper.

4. In another bowl, mix tomato sauce and Italian seasoning.

5. Spoon a thin layer of tomato sauce into bottom of the slow cooker. Top with about one-third of the eggplant slices, and then one-third of the egg/cheese mixture, and finally one-third of the remaining tomato sauce mixture.

6. Repeat those layers twice, ending with seasoned tomato sauce.

7. Cover. Cook on High for 4 hours. Allow to rest for 15 minutes before serving.

Quick-and-Easy Meatless Lasagna

Rhonda Freed, Lowville, NY

Makes 6 servings

Prep. Time: 10 minutes ⚜ *Cooking Time: 3–4 hours* ⚜ *Ideal slow-cooker size: 4-qt.*

28-oz. jar spaghetti sauce, your choice of flavors

6–7 uncooked lasagna noodles

2 cups shredded mozzarella cheese, *divided*

15 oz. ricotta cheese

¼ cup grated Parmesan cheese

1. Spread one-fourth of the sauce in the bottom of a slow cooker.

2. Lay 2 noodles, broken into 1-inch pieces, over the sauce.

3. In a bowl, mix together 1½ cups mozzarella, the ricotta, and the Parmesan.

4. Spoon half of the cheese mixture onto the noodles and spread out to the edges.

5. Spoon in one-third of the remaining sauce, and then 2 more broken noodles.

6. Spread the remaining cheese mixture over top, then one-half the remaining sauce and all the remaining noodles.

7. Finish with the remaining sauce.

8. Cover and cook on Low for 3 to 4 hours, or until noodles are tender and cheeses are melted.

9. Add ½ cup mozzarella cheese over the top, cover, and cook until cheese melts.

Maple-Glazed Salmon

Jenelle Miller, Marion, SD

Makes 6 servings

Prep. Time: 10 minutes   *Grilling Time: 8–9 minutes*

Nonstick cooking spray
2 tsp. paprika
2 tsp. chili powder
½ tsp. ground cumin
½ tsp. brown sugar
1 tsp. kosher salt, *optional*
6 4-oz. salmon fillets
1 Tbsp. maple syrup

1. Spray a grill rack with nonstick cooking spray. Heat the grill to medium.

2. In a small bowl, combine the paprika, chili powder, cumin, and brown sugar.

3. Sprinkle the fillets with salt, if using. Rub with the paprika mixture.

4. Place the fish on the grill rack. Grill for 7 minutes.

5. Drizzle the fish with maple syrup.

6. Grill for 1 to 2 minutes more, or until the fish flakes easily when tested with a fork.

CHICKEN

Chicken Baked with Red Onions, Potatoes, and Rosemary

Kristine Stalter, Iowa City, IA

Makes 8 servings

Prep. Time: 10–15 minutes ⚶ *Baking Time: 45–60 minutes*

2 red onions, each cut into 10 wedges

1¼ lb. new potatoes, unpeeled and cut into chunks

2 garlic bulbs, separated into cloves, unpeeled

Salt to taste

Pepper to taste

3 tsp. extra-virgin olive oil

2 Tbsp. balsamic vinegar

5 sprigs rosemary

8 chicken thighs, skin removed

1. Spread the onions, potatoes, and garlic in single layer over the bottom of a large roasting pan so that they will crisp and brown.

2. Season with salt and pepper.

3. Pour over the oil and balsamic vinegar and add rosemary, leaving some sprigs whole and stripping the leaves off the rest.

4. Toss the vegetables and seasonings together.

5. Tuck the chicken pieces among the vegetables.

6. Bake at 400°F for 45 to 60 minutes, or until the chicken and vegetables are cooked through.

7. Transfer to a big platter or take to the table in the roasting pan.

That's Amore Chicken Cacciatore

Carol Sherwood, Batavia, NY

Makes 6 servings

Prep. Time: 20 minutes 🦴 Cooking Time: 7–9 hours 🦴 Ideal slow-cooker size: 6-qt.

6 boneless, skinless chicken breast
halves, *divided*

28-oz. jar low-sugar, low-sodium
spaghetti sauce

2 green peppers, chopped

1 onion, minced

2 Tbsp. minced garlic

1. Place a layer of chicken in a slow cooker.

2. Mix the remaining ingredients together in a bowl. Spoon half of the sauce over the first layer of chicken.

3. Add the remaining breast halves. Top with the remaining sauce.

4. Cover and cook on Low for 7 to 9 hours, or until the chicken is tender but not dry.

Serving Suggestion:

Serve with the cooked spaghetti or other pasta.

Chicken Parmesan

Jessalyn Wantland, Napoleon, OH

Makes 4 servings

Prep. Time: 10 minutes   *Baking Time: 45 minutes*

I egg, beaten

¾ cup Italian-seasoned bread crumbs

4 boneless, skinless chicken breast halves, about 6 oz. each

25-oz. jar pasta sauce

I cup shredded Parmesan cheese

1. Grease a 7×11-inch baking dish.

2. Place the egg in a shallow bowl.

3. Place the bread crumbs in another shallow bowl.

4. Dip each piece of the chicken in the egg, and then in bread crumbs.

5. Place the coated chicken in the prepared baking dish.

6. Bake at 400°F for 30 minutes.

7. Spoon the pasta sauce over the chicken.

8. Top evenly with the cheese.

9. Bake for another 15 minutes, or until heated through and the cheese is melted.

Honey-Glazed Chicken

OVEN

Laura R. Showalter, Dayton, VA

Makes 6–8 servings

Prep. Time: 10–20 minutes ♣ *Baking Time: 1½ hours*

3 lb. chicken pieces

5⅓ Tbsp. (⅓ cup) butter, melted

⅓ cup honey

2 Tbsp. prepared mustard

1 tsp. salt

1 tsp. curry powder, *optional*

1. Place the chicken skin-side up in a 9×13-inch baking dish. (The dish is just as tasty if you remove the skin from the chicken!)

2. In a small bowl, combine the remaining ingredients. Pour over the chicken.

3. Bake uncovered at 350°F for 1 hour. Baste every 15 to 20 minutes. Cover and continue baking for 30 minutes, or until the chicken is tender and the juices run clear when pierced with a sharp fork.

Tip:

If you are unable to baste the chicken while baking, double the sauce so that it almost covers the chicken.

Jalapeño Chicken

Hope Comerford, Clinton Township, MI

Makes 4–6 servings

Prep. Time: 5 minutes   &   Cooking Time: 40–45 minutes

5 Tbsp. butter or coconut oil

6–8 chicken thighs or legs, or a combination of the two

10½ oz. jalapeño jelly (hot or mild depending on the spiciness you like)

2 Tbsp. minced onion

½ tsp. ginger

1 tsp. garlic powder

1 Tbsp. soy sauce or Liquid Aminos

1. In a frying pan, melt the butter and sear the chicken on both sides over medium-high heat.

2. In a small bowl, mix the jalapeño jelly, minced onion, ginger, garlic powder, and soy sauce. Pour this mixture over the chicken. Cover and cook on medium-low heat for 35 minutes, flipping occasionally.

3. Uncover and turn the heat up to medium-high. Baste the chicken and flip it frequently for 5–10 minutes more.

Easy Chicken Cordon Bleu

OVEN

Sharon Miller, Holmesville, OH

Makes 4 servings

Prep. Time: 15 minutes ❧ Cooking Time: 45–60 minutes

4 large boneless, skinless chicken breast halves, each about 8 oz. in weight

½–1 cup Italian-seasoned dry bread crumbs

4 large slices Swiss cheese

4 slices deli ham

1. Grease a 9×13-inch baking dish.

2. Pound each chicken breast to about ¼-inch to ½-inch thickness.

3. Place the bread crumbs in a shallow bowl.

4. Dredge each chicken piece in the bread crumbs, coating each side.

5. Lay a slice of Swiss cheese and a slice of ham on each chicken breast.

6. Tightly roll up each layered breast.

7. Holding the roll firmly, reroll in crumbs.

8. Stick 2 sturdy toothpicks through each roll to maintain its shape.

9. Place in a baking dish. Cover with foil.

10. Bake at 350°F for 30 minutes.

11. Remove the foil. Bake for an additional 15 minutes.

Tips:

1. The size of chicken breasts varies widely. If you're using extra-large breasts, 2 slices of ham and cheese per breast makes the dish even tastier. Match up chicken size with cheese and ham sizes as well as you can.

2. If the cheese is too "exposed" instead of being enclosed in the bundle, it melts outside the bundle.

Oven-Fried Chicken

OVEN

Eleanor Larson, Glen Lyon, PA

Makes 8 servings

Prep. Time: 5–10 minutes ⚜ *Baking Time: 1 hour*

½ cup flour

¼ tsp. paprika

½ tsp. salt

8 boneless, skinless chicken thighs, each about 6 oz.

1 stick (8 Tbsp.) butter, melted, *divided*

1. Grease a 9×13-inch baking dish well.

2. In a plastic bag, combine the flour, paprika, and salt.

3. Drop the chicken into the bag, one piece at a time. Shake to coat well.

4. Place the coated pieces of chicken in the baking dish.

5. Pour half of the melted butter evenly over the chicken.

6. Bake at 375°F for 30 minutes.

7. Turn each piece over.

8. Pour remaining butter evenly over chicken.

9. Return to oven. Bake an additional 30 minutes.

Tip:

You can double this for a larger group.

Baked Chicken Fingers

OVEN

Lori Rohrer, Washington Boro, PA

Makes 6 servings

Prep. Time: 20 minutes ⚬ *Baking Time: 20 minutes*

1½ cups fine, dry bread crumbs

½ cup grated Parmesan cheese

1½ tsp. salt

1 Tbsp. dried thyme

1 Tbsp. dried basil

7 boneless, skinless chicken breast halves, cut into 1½-inch slices

½ cup butter, melted

1. In a shallow bowl, combine the bread crumbs, cheese, salt, and herbs. Mix well.

2. Dip the chicken pieces in the butter, and then into the crumb mixture, coating well.

3. Place the coated chicken on a greased baking sheet in a single layer.

4. Bake at 400°F for 20 minutes.

Variations:

1. In Step 1 use 1 Tbsp. garlic powder, 1 Tbsp. chives, 2 tsp. Italian seasoning, 2 tsp. parsley, ½ tsp. onion salt, ½ tsp. pepper, and 1/4 tsp. salt.

—Ruth Miller, Wooster, OH

2. Use boneless, skinless chicken thighs, and do not cut them into slices. Bake at 350°F for 20 minutes. Turn chicken. Bake for an additional 20 minutes.

—Eleanor Larson, Glen Lyon, PA

Juicy Orange Chicken

Andrea Maher, Dunedin, FL

Makes 6 servings

Prep. Time: 10 minutes ⚘ *Cooking Time: 3–8 hours* ⚘ *Ideal slow-cooker size: 5- or 6-qt.*

18–24 oz. boneless, skinless chicken breast, cut into small pieces

1 cup orange juice, no additives

¼ cup honey

6 small oranges, peeled and sliced

¼ cup Liquid Aminos

1. In a slow cooker, combine all the ingredients.

2. Cover and cook on High for 3 to 4 hours or on Low for 6 to 8 hours.

Serving suggestion:

Serve over cooked brown rice.

Lemon Chicken

Judi Manos, West Islip, NY

Makes 4 servings

Prep. Time: 10–15 minutes 🪢 *Baking Time: 45–50 minutes*

¼ cup zesty Italian dressing

½ cup water

1 Tbsp. honey

1½ lb. bone-in chicken legs and thighs

1 lb. new potatoes, quartered, *optional*

5 cloves garlic, peeled

1 lemon, cut in 8 wedges

1 tsp. dried rosemary, *optional*

1. In a mixing bowl, blend together the dressing, water, and honey.

2. Arrange the chicken, potatoes (if using), and garlic in a well-greased 9×13-inch baking dish.

3. Drizzle with the dressing mixture.

4. Situate the lemon wedges and rosemary, if using, among the chicken and the potatoes, if using.

5. Bake at 400°F for 45 to 50 minutes, or until the chicken is done and potatoes are tender. (Temperature probe inserted into center of chicken should register 165°F.)

6. Serve the lemon wedges as garnish if you wish.

Variation:

For more flavor, use ½ cup of chicken broth instead of water.

Chicken Bruschetta Bake

Krista Hershberger, Elverson, PA

Makes 6 servings

Prep. Time: 15 minutes ⚓ *Cooking/Baking Time: 60 minutes*

1½ lb. boneless, skinless chicken breasts, cut into cubes

1 tsp. Italian seasoning

28-oz. can Italian-style stewed tomatoes, well drained

¾ cup shredded mozzarella cheese

6-oz. pkg. stuffing mix for chicken

1½ cups water

1. Place the chicken in a lightly greased 9×13-inch baking dish. Sprinkle with the Italian seasoning.

2. Spread the tomatoes over the top.

3. Sprinkle with the cheese.

4. In a mixing bowl, combine the stuffing mix with the water. Spoon over the ingredients in the baking dish.

5. Cover and bake for 30 minutes. Remove cover and bake for 30 more minutes.

Chicken and Broccoli Bake

Jan Rankin, Millersville, PA

Makes 12–16 servings

Prep. Time: 15 minutes ⚮ *Baking Time: 30 minutes*

2 10¾-oz. cans cream of chicken soup

2½ cups milk, *divided*

16-oz. bag frozen chopped broccoli, thawed and drained

3 cups cooked, chopped chicken breast

2 cups buttermilk baking mix

1. In a large mixing bowl, mix the soup and 1 cup milk together until smooth.

2. Stir in the broccoli and chicken.

3. Pour into a well-greased 9×13-inch baking dish.

4. In a mixing bowl, combine 1½ cups milk and the baking mix.

5. Spoon the baking mixture evenly over the top of the chicken-broccoli mixture.

6. Bake at 450°F for 30 minutes.

Chicken Alfredo

Erma Martin, East Earl, PA

Makes 4 servings

Prep. Time: 15 minutes   Cooking/Baking Time: 15–20 minutes

8-oz. pkg. cream cheese, cubed

¾ cup milk, *divided*

½ tsp. garlic powder

Salt to taste

Pepper to taste

4 skinless, boneless, chicken breast halves, cooked and diced

1. Ina skillet over medium heat, melt the cream cheese in about ⅓ cup of the milk, stirring until smooth.

2. Add the remaining milk, the garlic powder, the salt, and the pepper. Cook for about 3 minutes until thickened.

3. Add the diced chicken and cook until the chicken is well heated, about 3 minutes.

4. Serve over half a pound (dry) cooked fettuccine or other pasta.

Variation:

Add 2–3 cups thawed chopped broccoli to Step 3. Extend cooking time for that step to 5–7 minutes.

Tip:

Begin heating the cooking water for the fettuccine when you begin Step 1.

Baked Macaroni

Ann Good, Perry, NY

Makes 12 servings

Prep. Time: 5 minutes   Baking Time: 3 hours

¾ stick (6 Tbsp.) butter, melted

3 cups uncooked macaroni

2 qts. milk

4 cups shredded cheese of your choice

2 tsp. salt

½ tsp. pepper

1. In large bowl, mix together the butter, macaroni, milk, cheese, salt, and pepper.

2. Pour the mixture into a greased 9×13-inch casserole dish.

3. Cover. Bake at 225°F for 2¾ hours.

4. Remove the cover. Bake for 15 minutes longer to brown the dish.

PORK

Brown Sugar and Dijon-Marinated Pork Tenderloin

CHILLED · GRILL

J. B. Miller, Indianapolis, IN

Makes 4–6 servings

Prep. Time: 5 minutes ❧ Marinating Time: 2–3 hours ❧ Grilling Time: 15 minutes

½ cup soy sauce

¼ cup sherry vinegar

½ tsp. Dijon mustard

¼ cup brown sugar

2-lb. pork tenderloin

1. In a large ziplock bag, combine the soy sauce, vinegar, mustard, and brown sugar to make the marinade.

2. Place the tenderloin in the marinade and close the bag. Surround the meat with marinade, and then place in refrigerator for 2 to 3 hours.

3. Heat a grill to medium-high. Remove the tenderloin from the bag, patting it dry.

4. Grill the tenderloin until desired doneness, 160°F for medium. Thinly slice the meat into medallions and serve.

Tips:

1. Be sure the grill is hot before placing the tenderloin on the grill. The tenderloin should have a thin crisp crust.

2. This is especially good served with garlic mashed potatoes or polenta.

Pork Chops with Apple Pie Filling and Stuffing

Arlene M. Kopp, Lineboro, MD

Makes 6 servings

Prep. Time: 15 minutes & *Cooking Time: 2–3 hours* & *Ideal slow-cooker size: oval 6- or 7-qt.*

4 large baking apples, cored and sliced, peeled or unpeeled

¼ cup brown sugar

1 tsp. cinnamon

Salt to taste

Pepper to taste

6 (¾-inch-thick) bone-in, blade-cut pork chops

1. Grease the interior of a slow-cooker crock.

2. Scatter the apple slices over bottom of crock.

3. Sprinkle with the brown sugar and cinnamon.

4. Salt and pepper each chop on both sides. Place on top of the apples.

5. Cover. Cook on Low for 2 to 3 hours, or until an instant-read thermometer registers 140°F to 145°F.

6. Serve on a platter, topped with apples.

Cranberry-Glazed Pork Roast

Cova Rexroad, Kingsville, MD

Makes 6 servings

Prep. Time: 15 minutes ❧ *Roasting Time: 2 hours* ❧ *Standing Time: 25–30 minutes*

2½–3-lb. pork roast
1 tsp. salt
¼–½ tsp. pepper
16-oz. can whole berry cranberry sauce
½ cup orange juice
¼ cup brown sugar

1. Rub the pork roast with salt and pepper. Bake uncovered at 350°F for 1½ hours.

2. Meanwhile, in a small saucepan, combine the cranberry sauce, orange juice, and brown sugar. Cook over low heat until the mixture comes to a boil, making a thin sauce.

3. After the meat has roasted, brush ¼ of the sauce over the roast and bake uncovered for another 30 minutes.

4. Remove the roast from the pan and place it on a serving platter. Cover with foil and allow to stand for 25–30 minutes. Slice thinly and serve with the remaining sauce.

Variation:

For the glaze, use ¼ cup honey, 1 tsp. grated orange peel, ⅛ tsp. cloves, and ⅛ tsp. nutmeg, instead of orange juice and brown sugar.

—Chris Peterson, Green Bay, WI

Raspberry Balsamic Pork Chops

Hope Comerford, Clinton Township, MI

Makes 4–6 servings

Prep. Time: 5 minutes   Cooking Time: 7–8 hours   Ideal slow-cooker size: 3-qt.

4–5 lb. thick-cut pork chops

¼ cup raspberry balsamic vinegar

2 Tbsp. olive oil

½ tsp. kosher salt

½ tsp. garlic powder

¼ tsp. basil

¼ cup water

1. Place the pork chops in the slow cooker.

2. In a small bowl, mix together the remaining ingredients. Pour over the pork chops.

3. Cover and cook on Low for 7 to 8 hours.

Carnitas

Hope Comerford, Clinton Township, MI

Makes 12 servings

Prep. Time: 10 minutes ⚜ *Cooking Time: 10–12 hours* ⚜ *Ideal slow-cooker size: 4-qt.*

2-lb. pork shoulder roast

1½ tsp. kosher salt

½ tsp. pepper

2 tsp. cumin

5 cloves garlic, minced

1 tsp. oregano

3 bay leaves

2 cups low-sodium chicken stock

2 Tbsp. lime juice

1 tsp. lime zest

1. Place the pork shoulder roast in the slow-cooker crock.

2. In a bowl, mix together the salt, pepper, cumin, garlic, and oregano. Rub the mixture onto the pork roast.

3. Place the bay leaves around the pork roast, then pour in the chicken stock around the roast, being careful not to wash off the spices.

4. Cover and cook on Low for 10–12 hours.

5. Remove the roast with a slotted spoon, as well as the bay leaves. Shred the pork between 2 forks, then replace the shredded pork in the crock and stir.

6. Add the lime juice and lime zest to the crock and stir.

7. Serve on warmed white corn tortillas.

Tender Tasty Ribs

Carol Eveleth, Cheyenne, WY

Makes 2–3 servings

Prep. Time: 5 minutes ⚓ *Cooking Time: 35 minutes* ⚓ *Setting: Manual*
Pressure: High ⚓ *Release: Natural*

2 tsp. salt

2 tsp. black pepper

1 tsp. garlic powder

1 tsp. onion powder

1 slab baby back ribs

1 cup water

1 cup barbecue sauce, *divided*

1. In a bowl, mix the salt, pepper, garlic powder, and onion powder together. Rub the seasoning mixture on both sides of the slab of ribs. Cut the slab in half if it's too big for your Instant Pot.

2. Pour the water into the inner pot of the Instant Pot. Place the ribs into the pot, drizzle with ¼ cup of sauce, and secure the lid. Make sure the vent is set to sealing.

3. Set it to Manual for 25 minutes. It will take a few minutes to heat up and seal the vent. When cook time is up, let it sit 5 minutes, then release steam by turning valve to venting. Turn oven on to broil (or heat your grill) while you're waiting for the 5-minute resting time.

4. Remove the ribs from the Instant Pot and place them on a baking sheet. Slather on both sides with the remaining ¾ cup sauce.

5. Place under broiler (or on grill) for 5 to 10 minutes, watching carefully so it doesn't burn. Remove and brush with a bit more sauce. Pull apart and dig in!

Cordon Bleu Stromboli

Melody Baum, Greencastle, PA

Makes 6 servings

Prep. Time: 15 minutes   ♣   Rising Time: 20 minutes
Cooking/Baking Time: 25–30 minutes   ♣   Standing Time: 10 minutes

1 loaf frozen bread dough, thawed (see package directions)

2 Tbsp. butter

8 oz. thinly sliced deli ham

½ cup shredded Swiss cheese

5 oz. thinly sliced deli turkey

1. Roll the bread dough into an 8×10-inch rectangle on a baking sheet.

2. Spread with the butter. Top with a layer of ham, followed by a layer of cheese, and finally a layer of turkey.

3. Roll up, jelly-roll style, starting with the long side. Pinch the seam to seal and tuck the ends under.

4. Place seam-side down on a greased baking sheet. Set in a warm place. Cover with a tea towel, and let rise for 20 minutes.

5. Bake at 350°F for 25 to 30 minutes, or until golden brown.

6. Allow to stand for 10 minutes before slicing.

Italian Sausage and Potatoes

Maryann Markano, Wilmington, DE

Makes 4 servings

Prep. Time: 20 minutes ☙ *Cooking/Baking Time: 30–35 minutes*

1 lb. sweet or hot Italian sausage, cut on the diagonal in 1½-inch lengths

1 lb. small red potatoes, each cut in half

1 large onion, cut into 12 wedges

2 red or yellow bell peppers, cut into strips

1 Tbsp. olive oil

1. Preheat the oven to 450°F.

2. In a large bowl or a plastic bag, combine all the ingredients. Toss to coat the meat and vegetables with oil.

3. Pour the mixture onto a large, lightly greased jelly-roll pan.

4. Roast for 30 to 35 minutes, or until the potatoes are fork-tender and the sausages are lightly browned. Stir halfway through cooking.

Easy Pot Roast and Vegetables

Tina Houk, Clinton, MO
Arlene Wines, Newton, KS

Makes 6 servings

Prep. Time: 20 minutes ✂ Cooking Time: 35 minutes ✂ Setting: Manual
Pressure: High ✂ Release: Natural

3–4 lb. chuck roast, trimmed of fat and cut into serving-sized chunks

4 medium potatoes, cubed, unpeeled

4 medium carrots, sliced, or 1 lb. baby carrots

2 celery ribs, sliced thin

1 envelope dry onion soup mix

3 cups water

1. In an Instant Pot, combine the pot roast chunks with the potatoes, carrots, and celery.

2. Mix together the onion soup mix and water and pour over the contents of the Instant Pot.

3. Secure the lid and make sure the vent is set to sealing. Set the Instant Pot to Manual mode for 35 minutes. Let the pressure release naturally when the cook time is up.

Roast Beef and Mushrooms

Gladys M. High, Ephrata, PA

Makes 4–6 servings

Prep. Time: 10 minutes ♣ Cooking Time: 8–10 hours ♣ Ideal slow-cooker size: 3-qt.

3-lb. boneless chuck roast

¼ lb. fresh mushrooms, sliced, or 4-oz. can mushroom stems and pieces, drained

1 cup water

1 envelope dry brown gravy mix

1 envelope dry Italian dressing mix

1. Place the roast in a slow cooker.

2. Top with the mushrooms.

3. In a small bowl, mix together the water, dry gravy mix, and dry Italian dressing mix. Pour over the roast and mushrooms.

4. Cover and cook on Low for 8 to 10 hours, or until the meat is tender but not dry.

Herb-Marinated Steak

Linda E. Wilcox, Blythewood, SC

Makes 4 servings

Prep. Time: 10 minutes ⚜ Marinating Time: 6–8 hours
Broiling Time: 12–18 minutes ⚜ Standing Time: 10 minutes

¼ cup chopped onion
2 Tbsp. fresh parsley
2 Tbsp. balsamic vinegar
1 Tbsp. olive oil
2 tsp. Dijon-style mustard
1 tsp. garlic powder
1-lb. London broil, or chuck steak

1. In a bowl, combine the onion, parsley, vinegar, oil, mustard, and garlic.

2. Place the London broil or chuck steak in a sturdy plastic bag. Add the onion mixture, spreading it on both sides of the meat. Close the bag securely.

3. Place the filled bag in a long dish in case of any leaks. Marinate in the refrigerator for 6 to 8 hours, or overnight. Turn it over at least once while marinating.

4. Pour off the marinade. Place the steak on a rack in the broiler pan so the meat is about 5 inches from the heat source. Broil for about 6 to 8 minutes on each side for rare or 9 minutes on each side for medium.

5. When finished broiling, allow meat to stand for 10 minutes.

6. Carve diagonally across the grain into thin slices.

Variation:

Use fresh garlic instead of garlic powder.

Tip:

You can grill the steak rather than broil it.

Beef and Pepperoncini Hoagies

Donna Treloar, Muncie, IN

Makes 10 servings

Prep. Time: 15 minutes ⚬ *Cooking Time: 8–10 hours on Low* ⚬ *Ideal slow-cooker size: 5- or 6-qt.*

3–5 lb. boneless chuck roast (inexpensive cuts work fine)

1 tsp. garlic powder or minced garlic

Salt to taste

Pepper to taste

16-oz. jar of pepperoncini peppers, mild or medium, depending on your preference

Hoagie rolls or buns of your choice

20 slices provolone cheese

1. Grease the interior of a slow-cooker crock.

2. Trim fat from the roast.

3. Salt and pepper the roast to taste, holding over the crock.

4. If using garlic powder, sprinkle on all sides of the beef over the crock. Place the beef in the crock.

5. If using minced garlic, scatter it over the beef in the crock.

6. If the pepperoncini peppers are whole and have stems, remove the peppers from the jar and cut them up. Reserve the liquid.

7. Scatter the chopped peppers over the meat.

8. Pour the liquid from the peppers down alongside of the crock interior so you don't wash off the seasonings.

9. Cover. Cook on Low for 7½ to 9½ hours, or until the beef registers 160°F on an instant-read meat thermometer when stuck in center of roast.

10. Lift the roast into a big bowl and shred with 2 forks.

11. Stir the shredded meat back into the juices in the crock.

12. Cover. Cook for another 30 minutes on Low.

13. When ready to serve, use a slotted spoon to drain the meat well.

14. Spoon well-drained meat onto a hoagie roll and top each sandwich with 2 slices of cheese.

Variations:

1. Use fresh garlic instead of garlic powder.

2. You can add chopped onions to Step 7.

3. Add a package of dry Italian dressing mix or Lipton Onion Soup mix and a cup or two of beef broth to steps 7 and 8.

Un-Stuffed Peppers

STOVETOP

Pat Bechtel, Dillsburg, PA
Sharon Miller, Holmesville, OH

Makes 6 servings

Prep. Time: 10–12 minutes ⚬ *Cooking/Baking Time: 25 minutes*

1 lb. ground beef

1 lb. 10-oz. jar spaghetti sauce

2 Tbsp. barbecue sauce, *optional*

2 large green peppers (3–4 cups),
coarsely chopped

1¼ cups water

1 cup instant rice

1. In a 12-inch nonstick skillet, brown the ground beef. Drain off the drippings.

2. Stir in all the remaining ingredients. Bring to a boil over high heat.

3. Reduce the heat to medium-low and cook, covered, for 20 minutes, or until the liquid is absorbed and the rice is tender.

Variation:

Instead of spaghetti sauce and water, substitute 4 cups tomato juice or V-8 juice.

—Sharon Miller, Holmesville, OH

Oven Enchiladas

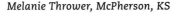

Melanie Thrower, McPherson, KS

Makes 8 servings

Prep. Time: 15 minutes ⚶ *Cooking/Baking Time: 30 minutes*

1 lb. ground beef

16 corn tortillas

2 medium yellow onions, chopped

2 cups shredded Mexican cheese

2 16-oz. cans green or red enchilada sauce

1. In a skillet, brown the ground beef. Drain off the drippings.

2. In a nonstick pan, heat the tortillas to make them flexible.

3. Fill each tortilla with browned beef, topped with onion. Roll up, tuck in the sides, and continue rolling. Place side by side on a baking sheet with sides.

4. Sprinkle the cheese over the top of the filled enchiladas. Pour the sauce over the top.

5. Cover with aluminum foil. Bake at 375°F for 30 minutes.

Tip:

Serve with dishes of sour cream, salsa, and guacamole as optional toppings.

BBQ Meat Loaf

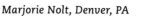

Marjorie Nolt, Denver, PA

Makes 10 servings

Prep. Time: 30 minutes ♣ Cooking Time: 5–6 hours ♣ Ideal slow-cooker size: oval 6-qt.

2 lb. lean ground beef

1 lb. lean ground pork

½ cup finely chopped onion

½ cup almond, or all-purpose, flour

1 tsp. salt

1 tsp. black pepper

1 tsp. garlic powder

2 large eggs

1 cup of your favorite barbecue sauce, *optional*

1. Grease the interior of a slow-cooker crock.

2. Make a tinfoil sling for the slow cooker so you can lift the cooked meat loaf out easily. Begin by folding a strip of tinfoil accordion-fashion so that it's about 1½ inches to 2 inches wide, and long enough to fit from the top edge of the crock, down inside and up the other side, plus a 2-inch overhang on each side of the cooker. Make a second strip exactly like the first.

3. Place one strip in the crock, running from end to end. Place the second strip in the crock, running from side to side. The 2 strips should form a cross in the bottom of the crock.

4. In a large bowl, mix all ingredients together, except barbecue sauce. Mix well with your hands until fully combined.

5. Place the loaf into the crock, centering it where the 2 foil strips cross.

6. Cover. Cook on Low for 3 to 4 hours.

7. Thirty minutes before the end of the cooking time, brush the top and sides of the loaf with about ⅓ cup of barbecue sauce, if using.

8. Use the foil handles to lift the meat loaf out of the crock and onto a serving platter. Let it stand for 10 to 15 minutes to allow the meat to gather its juices.

9. Slice and serve with the remaining barbecue sauce, if using.

Saucy Tacos

Sarah Herr, Goshen, IN

Makes 8 servings

Prep. Time: 20 minutes ⚜ Cooking Time: 6–8 hours ⚜ Ideal slow-cooker size: 4-qt.

2 lb. flank steak

1 green bell pepper, chopped

1 onion, chopped

1 cup salsa (I use peach flavored, which is less tomatoey)

2 Tbsp., or 1 envelope, taco seasoning

1. Grease the interior of a slow-cooker crock.

2. Place the steak in the crock.

3. In a bowl, mix all the other ingredients. Spoon over meat.

4. Cover. Cook for 6 to 8 hours on Low, or until an instant-read meat thermometer registers 140°F to 145°F when stuck in the center.

5. Shred the meat with 2 forks or slice thinly. Mix with the vegetables and juice.

6. Serve with tortillas or taco shells or drain and include the meat in a taco salad.

SIDE DISHES

Ranch Potato Cubes

Charlotte Shaffer, East Earl, PA

Makes 8 servings

Prep. Time: 20 minutes ⚓ *Baking Time: 1 hour 10 minutes*

6 medium potatoes, cut into ½-inch cubes

½ stick (4 Tbsp.) butter, cubed

1 cup sour cream

1 packet ranch salad dressing mix

1 cup (4 oz.) shredded cheddar cheese

1. In a greased 7×11-inch baking dish, dot the potatoes with butter.

2. Cover. Bake at 350°F for 1 hour.

3. Combine the sour cream and salad dressing mix.

4. Spoon over the potatoes. Sprinkle with the cheese.

5. Bake uncovered for 10 minutes until the cheese is melted.

Rosemary Roasted Potatoes

Pamela Pierce, Annville, PA

Makes 8 servings

Prep. Time: 10 minutes & Baking Time: 45–60 minutes

8 medium red potatoes, scrubbed,
dried, and cut into wedges

3 Tbsp. olive oil

1 tsp. crushed dried rosemary

1 tsp. crushed dried thyme

½ tsp. salt

⅛ tsp. pepper

1. Toss the potato wedges in oil.

2. Place the potato wedges in a shallow roasting pan and sprinkle evenly with the rosemary, thyme, salt, and pepper. Stir.

3. Roast in 375°F oven for 45 to 60 minutes, stirring every 10 to 15 minutes, until golden and fork-tender.

Healthy Sweet Potato Fries

Gladys M. High, Ephrata, PA

Makes 4 servings

Prep. Time: 15 minutes   *Roasting Time: 30 minutes*

Organic olive oil cooking spray

2 large sweet potatoes, peeled and cut into wedges

¼ tsp. salt

¼ tsp. black pepper

Oregano, *optional*

Thyme, *optional*

Rosemary, *optional*

Garlic powder, *optional*

1. Preheat the oven to 400°F.

2. Coat a baking sheet with organic olive oil cooking spray.

3. Arrange the potato wedges on the prepared baking sheet in a single layer. Coat with cooking spray.

4. Sprinkle the potatoes with salt, pepper, and any additional seasonings of your choice.

5. Roast for 30 minutes, or until tender and golden brown.

Rice Guiso

Cynthia Hockman-Chupp, Canby, OR

Makes 3–6 servings

Prep. Time: 5 minutes ❧ Cooking Time: 15 minutes ❧ Setting: Rice
Pressure: High ❧ Release: Natural or Manual

1 Tbsp. oil (I prefer coconut)

1 onion, chopped

1 cup rice

1 tsp. salt

⅛ tsp. pepper

¼–½ cup chopped bell pepper, any color (or a variety of colors!)

1–1⅛ cups water

2 Tbsp. tomato paste

1. In the inner pot of an Instant Pot, stir all the ingredients to combine.

2. Secure the lid and make sure the vent is at sealing. Push the rice button and set for 15 minutes. Allow to cook.

3. Use manual release for a final product that is more moist; use natural release for a slightly drier rice. I prefer natural release for this rice.

Barbecued Baked Beans

SLOW COOKER

Anne Nolt, Thompsontown, PA

Makes 6–8 servings

Prep. Time: 15 minutes · *Cooking Time: 3 hours* · *Ideal slow-cooker size: 3-qt.*

- 6 slices uncooked bacon, cut into pieces
- 2 15-oz. cans pork and beans
- 1 tsp. dry mustard, or 1 Tbsp. prepared mustard
- ½ cup ketchup
- ¾ cup brown sugar

1. In a nonstick skillet, brown the bacon until it is crispy. Drain.

2. In a slow cooker, mix the bacon with all the remaining ingredients.

3. Cover and cook on High for 3 hours. Remove the cover during the last 30 minutes to allow some of the juice to cook off.

Green Bean and Mushroom Sauté

Louise Bodziony, Sunrise Beach, MO
Clara Yoder Byler, Hartville, OH

Makes 4 servings

Prep. Time: 10 minutes ☙ Cooking Time: 20 minutes

1 lb. fresh, or frozen, green beans

¾–1 cup sliced fresh mushrooms

2 Tbsp. butter

2–3 tsp. onion powder or garlic powder

4 slices bacon, cooked and crumbled, *optional*

1. Cook the green beans in water to cover, just until tender.

2. Meanwhile, in a skillet, sauté the mushrooms in the butter until tender.

3. Stir in the onion powder.

4. Drain the beans. Add them to the skillet and toss with the mushrooms and onion powder.

5. Place in a serving dish. Top with crumbled bacon, if using.

Holiday Green Beans

Joanne Kennedy, Plattsburgh, NY
Jean Ryan, Peru, NY

Makes 10 servings

Prep. Time: 10 minutes ☙ Cooking Time: 20 minutes

2 lb. (about 8 cups) fresh green beans
I large red onion, thinly sliced
3 cloves fresh garlic, minced
I tsp. olive oil
½ cup slivered almonds
Pepper to taste

1. In a saucepan, steam the beans until they are just slightly crisp.

2. In a large skillet, sauté the onion and garlic in olive oil for 3 minutes.

3. Add beans to the skillet. Sauté for 1 minute.

4. Add the slivered almonds and pepper to the beans. Toss them together and then serve.

Maple-Glazed Squash

OVEN

Jean Turner, Williams Lake, BC

Makes 6–8 servings

Prep. Time: 10–15 minutes ⚓ *Baking Time: 50–55 minutes*

2 acorn squash

Salt

Pepper

⅔ cup maple syrup

½ cup soft bread crumbs

½ stick (4 Tbsp.) butter, softened

1. Trim off the ends of the acorn squash, then cut crosswise into 1-inch slices. Discard the seeds.

2. Season the squash with salt and pepper.

3. In a large shallow baking pan, arrange a single layer of squash. Cover and bake at 350°F for 30 to 35 minutes.

4. In a small mixing bowl, combine the syrup, crumbs, and butter. Spread the mixture over the squash.

5. Bake uncovered for 15 to 20 minutes, basting occasionally.

Zucchini Casserole

Virginia R. Bender, Dover, DE

Makes 6 servings

Prep. Time: 30 minutes ⚘ *Baking Time: 1 hour*

4 cups grated fresh zucchini

1 medium onion, grated

2 Tbsp. flour

4 eggs

½–¾ cup grated cheddar cheese

Black pepper or other seasoning

Salt to taste, *optional*

1. Place the grated zucchini and onion into a lightly greased 2-qt. baking dish and mix together gently.

2. Sprinkle the flour over all.

3. In a mixing bowl, beat the eggs. Pour over all. Stir.

4. Sprinkle with the grated cheese, pepper, and salt, if using.

5. Bake uncovered at 350°F for 1 hour.

Broccoli with Garlic and Lemon

Jan Moore, Wellsville, KS
Leona Yoder, Hartville, OH

Makes 4–5 servings

Prep. Time: 10 minutes ❧ *Cooking Time: 10–15 minutes*

4½ cups fresh broccoli florets

¼–½ cup water

1 Tbsp. extra-virgin olive oil

1 garlic clove, crushed, or ½ tsp. jarred minced garlic

Juice and grated zest of ½ lemon

Grated Parmesan cheese, *optional*

1. In a large covered saucepan over medium-high heat, combine the broccoli and water and cook, stirring occasionally, for several minutes, until the broccoli is crisp-tender. Add more water if necessary to prevent scorching, but only a small amount.

2. Drain any excess liquid from the skillet. Push the broccoli to one side and add the olive oil and garlic to the other side. Cook for about 10 to 20 seconds, or until the garlic begins to turn color and smell fragrant.

3. Toss all together.

4. Stir in the lemon juice and zest.

5. When ready to serve, top with Parmesan cheese, if using.

Cheesy Cauliflower

Joan Erwin, Sparks, NV

Makes 4–5 servings

Prep. Time: 5–10 minutes ♨ Cooking Time: 10 minutes

I head cauliflower
I Tbsp. water
I cup mayonnaise
I Tbsp. prepared mustard
½ cup chopped green or red onions
I cup any combination of shredded Monterey Jack and cheddar cheeses

1. Place the whole cauliflower head in a microwavable glass baking dish. Add the water. Cover. Microwave on High for 9 minutes, until crisp-cooked.

2. Meanwhile, in a small bowl, combine the mayonnaise, mustard, and onions. Spread over the cooked cauliflower. Sprinkle with the cheese.

3. Cover and microwave on High for 1 minute, or until the cheese is melted.

Variation:

You may break the cauliflower into florets and proceed with Step 1.

Oven Brussels Sprouts

Gail Martin, Elkhart, IN

Makes 8 servings

Prep. Time: 15 minutes ❧ *Baking Time: 15–20 minutes*

1½ lb. Brussels sprouts, halved

¼ cup plus 2 Tbsp. olive oil

Juice of 1 lemon

½ tsp. salt

½ tsp. pepper

½ tsp. crushed red pepper flakes

1. In a large bowl, toss halved sprouts with 2 Tbsp. olive oil.

2. Place them on a single layer on a rimmed cookie sheet.

3. Roast the sprouts in the oven at 450°F, stirring twice, until crisp and lightly browned, about 15 to 20 minutes.

4. In a large bowl, whisk together ¼ cup oil and the lemon juice, salt, pepper, and crushed red pepper flakes.

5. Toss the sprouts with the dressing and serve.

Tip:

Don't overcook the sprouts.

Roasted Baby Carrots

Melanie Mohler, Ephrata, PA

Makes 4–5 servings

Prep. Time: 5–10 minutes ❧ *Cooking/Roasting Time: 10–15 minutes*

I lb. baby carrots
I Tbsp. olive oil
I Tbsp. dried dill weed
Sprinkle salt

1. Preheat the oven to 475°F.

2. If using thick baby carrots, slice them in half lengthwise. Otherwise leave as is.

3. In a large bowl, combine the olive oil and dill. Add the carrots and toss to coat.

4. In a 10×15-inch baking pan, spread the carrots in a single layer.

5. Roast, uncovered, for about 10 minutes or until the carrots are just tender, stirring once.

6. Sprinkle with salt before serving.

Roasted Potato Salad

Mary Puskar, Forest Hill, MD

Makes 10 servings

Prep. Time: 30 minutes ⚖ *Baking Time: 30–35 minutes*

Nonstick cooking spray
5 lb. potatoes, unpeeled, quartered
1 lb. bacon
2–3 chopped hard-cooked eggs
1 bunch scallions, chopped
16-oz. jar Miracle Whip salad dressing

1. In a baking pan sprayed with nonstick cooking spray, bake the potatoes at 425°F for 30 to 35 minutes, or until tender.

2. Meanwhile, in a large skillet or in the oven, cook the bacon until crisp. Drain the bacon. When it is cooled, crumble. Set aside.

3. In a large mixing bowl, mix all the ingredients. Toss well and serve.

Tortellini Summer Salad

Norma P. Zehr, Lowville, NY

Makes 4–6 servings

Prep. Time: 15 minutes   Cooking Time: 10 minutes   Cooling Time: 30 minutes

9-oz. pkg. cheese tortellini
1 cup julienned fully cooked ham
¾ cup frozen peas, thawed
½ cup Swiss cheese, cut in cubes
2 cups ranch dressing

1. Cook the tortellini according to package directions until done. Drain and cool.

2. In a large mixing bowl, combine all the ingredients and toss.

3. Chill until ready to serve.

Variation:

Add several tablespoons minced onion in Step 2 for extra flavor.

Sour Cream Cucumber Salad

Mary Jones, Marengo, OH

Makes 6 servings

Prep. Time: 20–30 minutes

3 medium cucumbers, sliced thinly
½ tsp. salt
½ cup finely chopped scallions
I Tbsp. white vinegar
Dash pepper, *optional*
¼ cup sour cream

1. In a glass bowl, sprinkle the cucumbers with salt. Let stand for 15 minutes. Drain the liquid.

2. Add the scallions, vinegar, and pepper.

3. Just before serving, stir in the sour cream.

Variation:

Use lemon juice instead of vinegar and make a dressing with sour cream, salt, lemon juice, and 2 tsp. sugar. Simply add the dressing to the cucumbers and onions, chilling 2 hours before serving.

—Joyce Shackelford, Green Bay, WI

Simple Broccoli Slaw

Hope Comerford, Clinton Township, MI

Makes 4 cups

Prep. Time: 5 minutes ⚘ *Chilling Time: 30 minutes*

4 cups broccoli slaw

Dressing:

¼ cup olive oil

¼ cup apple cider vinegar

2 Tbsp. sugar

½ tsp. mustard powder

½ tsp. garlic powder

½ tsp. onion powder

1. Place the slaw in a bowl. In another bowl, mix together all of the dressing ingredients. Pour this over the broccoli slaw.

2. Refrigerate for 30 minutes or longer.

Poppy Seed Coleslaw

Esther Becker, Gordonville, PA

Makes 8–10 servings

Prep. Time: 10–15 minutes ✣ Chilling Time: 1 hour

16-oz. bag tricolor coleslaw mix
8¼-oz. can mandarin oranges, drained
8-oz. can pineapple chunks, drained
½ cup poppy seed salad dressing
½ cup sour cream

1. In a large mixing bowl, combine the coleslaw mix, oranges, and pineapple.

2. In a small bowl, stir together the poppy seed dressing and sour cream.

3. Pour the dressing over the slaw. Mix and toss.

4. Chill in the refrigerator for an hour.

DESSERTS

Peanut Butter Cookies

OVEN

Juanita Lyndaker, Croghan, NY
Stacy Stoltzfus, Grantham, PA
Joleen Albrecht, Gladstone, MI
Doris Bachman, Putnam, IL

Makes 1–1½ dozen cookies

Prep. Time: 15 minutes ♨ Baking Time: 8–10 minutes per sheet

I cup peanut butter
I cup sugar, plus more for rolling
I egg

1. In a medium mixing bowl, mix the peanut butter, sugar, and egg to combine.

2. Break portions of dough off with a teaspoon and shape the portions into balls.

3. Roll each ball in granulated sugar.

4. Place the balls on a greased baking sheet. Press down with a fork, making a crisscross pattern.

5. Bake at 350°F for 8–10 minutes, or until golden brown.

Lemon Chocolate Chip Cookies

OVEN

Hope Comerford, Clinton Township, MI

Makes 24 cookies

Prep. Time: 10 minutes ❦ Baking Time: 15 minutes

I box lemon cake mix

2 eggs

½ cup vegetable oil or coconut oil

I cup white chocolate chips

1. Preheat the oven to 325°F.

2. In a large mixing bowl, mix together the lemon cake mix, eggs, and vegetable oil. Stir in the white chocolate chips.

3. On a greased cookie sheet or parchment-paper-lined cookie sheet, place 1½-tsp.-sized balls of dough 1 inch apart.

4. Bake for 15 minutes.

5. Let cool slightly, then place on a cooling rack.

Lemon Squares

Mary Kathryn Yoder, Harrisonville, MO

Makes 15 servings

Prep. Time: 10 minutes ⚶ *Baking Time: 30 minutes* ⚶ *Cooling Time: 1–2 hours*

1 box angel food cake mix
21-oz. can lemon pie filling
⅛ cup confectioners' sugar

1. In a large mixing bowl, use an electric mixer to mix the cake mix and pie filling together.

2. Pour the mixture into a lightly greased 9×13-inch baking pan.

3. Bake at 350°F for 30 minutes. Let cool.

4. Sprinkle confectioners' sugar over the top.

5. Cut into bars.

Peach Cobbler

OVEN

Eileen Eash, Carlsbad, NM
June S. Groff, Denver, PA
Sharon Wantland, Menomonee Falls, WI

Makes 10 servings

Prep. Time: 30 minutes ⚮ Baking Time: 60–70 minutes

8 cups sliced fresh, or frozen, peaches

1 stick (8 Tbsp.) butter, softened

¾ cup sugar

1 cup flour

Cinnamon sugar (¼ tsp. cinnamon mixed with ½ tsp. sugar)

1. Place the peaches in an ungreased 9×13-inch baking dish.

2. In a medium mixing bowl, cream the butter and sugar together, either with a spoon or an electric mixer.

3. Add the flour and mix well. Sprinkle over the peaches.

4. Top with the cinnamon sugar.

5. Bake at 325°F for 60 to 70 minutes, or until the top is golden brown.

6. Serve warm with milk or ice cream, if you wish.

Ultimate Apple Crisp

OVEN

Judi Manos, West Islip, NY

Makes 6–8 servings

Prep. Time: 15 minutes   *Cooking/Baking Time: 25 minutes*

6–8 apples (use baking apples if you can find them)

I cup brown sugar

I cup dry oats, quick or rolled (both work, but rolled have more texture)

I cup flour

I Tbsp. cinnamon

1½ sticks (12 Tbsp.) butter, melted

½ stick (4 Tbsp.) butter, cut in pieces

1. Core, peel if you want, and slice apples. Place the apples in a microwave- and oven-safe baking dish (a Pyrex-type pie plate works well).

2. In a separate bowl, mix together the brown sugar, oats, flour, and cinnamon. Add the melted butter and mix with a fork until thoroughly mixed.

3. Place the mixture on top of the apples. Microwave on High, uncovered, for 10 minutes. Let stand for 2 minutes.

4. Place the cut-up butter on top of the heated apple mixture.

5. Place in the oven and bake at 350°F for 15 minutes.

Fresh Peach Pie

Lavon Martins, Postville, IA
Darlene E. Miller, South Hutchinson, KS

Makes 6–8 servings

Prep. Time: 15 minutes ☙ Cooking Time: 10 minutes ☙ Chilling Time: 30 minutes

¾ cup sugar
½ tsp. salt
1 cup water
3 Tbsp. cornstarch
2 Tbsp. white corn syrup
3-oz. pkg. peach gelatin
4–6 peaches
9-inch baked piecrust

1. In a saucepan, combine the sugar, salt, water, cornstarch, and syrup. Cook until clear, stirring constantly.

2. Add the gelatin and stir until dissolved. Cool in the refrigerator for 30 minutes.

3. Slice the peaches. Place them in the piecrust.

4. Pour the filling over the peaches. Chill until ready to serve.

5. Serve with whipped cream or ice cream.

Variation:

Replace the peach gelatin with strawberry gelatin. And use 1 qt. strawberries, fresh or frozen, instead of the peaches.

—June S. Groff, Denver, PA

Note:

If you want to make your own crust, try this:

1½ cups flour
½ tsp. salt
1½ Tbsp. sugar
2 Tbsp. milk
½ cup oil

Mix all ingredients together in a mixing bowl. When blended, simply press into a 9-inch pie plate. Jag with a fork to keep it from buckling while baking. Bake at 350°F until golden brown. Cool thoroughly before filling with fruit.

—Darlene E. Miller, South Hutchinson, KS

Pineapple Upside-Down Cake

Vera M. Kuhns, Harrisonburg, VA

Makes 10 servings

Prep. Time: 20 minutes ⚜ *Cooking Time: 4–5 hours* ⚜ *Ideal slow-cooker size: 4-qt.*

½ cup butter, or margarine, melted

1 cup brown sugar

1 20-oz. can pineapple slices, drained, reserving juice

6–8 maraschino cherries

1 box dry yellow cake mix

1. In a bowl, combine the butter and brown sugar. Spread over the bottom of a well-greased slow-cooker crock.

2. Add the pineapple slices and place cherries in the center of each one.

3. Prepare the cake according to package directions, using the reserved pineapple juice for part of the liquid. Spoon the cake batter into the cooker over the top of the fruit.

4. Cover the cooker with 2 tea towels and then with its own lid. Cook on High for 1 hour, and then on Low for 3 to 4 hours.

5. Allow the cake to cool for 10 minutes. Then run a knife around the edge and invert the cake onto a large platter.

Instant Pot Dump Cake

Janie Steele, Moore, OK

Makes 8–10 servings

Prep. Time: 10 minutes & Cooking Time: 12 minutes & Setting: Manual
Pressure: High & Release: Manual

6 Tbsp. butter

1 box cake mix (I used spice cake)

2 20-oz. cans pie filling (I used apple)

1. In a bowl, mix the butter and dry cake mix. It will be clumpy.

2. Pour the pie filling into the inner pot of the Instant Pot.

3. Pour the dry mix over the top of the pie filling.

4. Secure the lid and make sure vent is at sealing. Cook for 12 minutes on Manual mode at high pressure.

5. Release pressure manually when the cook time is up and remove the lid to prevent condensation from getting into the cake.

6. Let stand for 5 to 10 minutes.

Serving suggestion:
Serve with ice cream.

Raspberry Angel Food Cake

Hope Comerford, Clinton Township, MI

Makes about 20 servings

Prep. Time: 1½ hours   Chilling Time: 1¼ hours

I cup boiling water

3-oz. pkg. raspberry gelatin

½ cup cold water

I pt. raspberries

8 oz. frozen whipped topping, thawed, *divided*

10-inch angel food cake

1. In a medium bowl, pour 1 cup of boiling water into the gelatin and stir until dissolved. Then, pour in ½ cup cold water.

2. Refrigerate for 1 hour.

3. Fold in most of the raspberries and ½ (4 oz.) of the whipped topping. (You'll want a few raspberries to decorate with at the end.)

4. Split the angel food cake into 3 layers. Spread ½ of the gelatin mixture over the bottom layer. Repeat this process once more, ending with the top layer.

5. Spread the remaining whipped topping over the cake and decorate with the remaining raspberries.

Blueberry Swirl Cake

Lori Lehman, Ephrata, PA

Makes 15 servings

Prep. Time: 15 minutes   *Baking Time: 30–40 minutes*

3-oz. pkg. cream cheese, softened
18¼-oz. box white cake mix
3 eggs
3 Tbsp. water
21-oz. can blueberry pie filling

1. In a large mixing bowl, beat the cream cheese until it is soft and creamy.

2. Stir in the dry cake mix, eggs, and water. Blend well with the cream cheese.

3. Pour into a greased 9×13-inch baking pan.

4. Pour the blueberry pie filling over the top of the batter.

5. Swirl the blueberries and batter with a knife by zigzagging through batter.

6. Bake at 350°F for 30 to 40 minutes, or until a tester inserted in the center comes out clean.

Dark Chocolate Lava Cake

Hope Comerford, Clinton Township, MI

Makes 8 servings

Prep. Time: 5–10 minutes ⚶ *Cook Time: 2–3 hours* ⚶ *Ideal slow-cooker size: 4-qt.*

5 eggs

I cup dark cocoa powder

⅔ cup maple syrup

⅔ cup dark chocolate, chopped into very fine pieces or shaved

Nonstick cooking spray

1. In a large mixing bowl, whisk the eggs and then slowly whisk in the cocoa powder, maple syrup, and dark chocolate.

2. Spray a slow-cooker crock with nonstick cooking spray.

3. Pour the egg/chocolate mixture into the crock.

4. Cover and cook on Low for 2 to 3 hours with some folded paper towel under the lid to collect condensation. It is done when the middle is set and bounces back up when touched.

Apple German Chocolate Cake

Sue Pennington, Bridgewater, VA

Makes 12–15 servings

Prep. Time: 10–15 minutes & Baking Time: 40–45 minutes

21-oz. can apple pie filling

18¼-oz. pkg. German chocolate cake mix

3 eggs

¾ cup coarsely chopped walnuts

½ cup miniature semisweet chocolate chips

1. Place the pie filling in a blender. Cover and process until the apples are in ¼-inch chunks.

2. Pour the processed pie filling into a mixing bowl.

3. Add the dry cake mix and eggs. Beat on medium speed for 5 minutes.

4. Pour into a greased 9×13-inch baking pan.

5. Sprinkle with the walnuts and chocolate chips.

6. Bake at 350°F for 40 to 45 minutes, or until a toothpick inserted in the center comes out clean. Cool completely on rack before cutting.

Easy Brownies

Donna Klaassen, Whitewater, KS

Makes 36 brownies

Prep. Time: 15 minutes ⚘ *Cooking/Baking Time: 25–30 minutes*

I stick butter (½ cup), softened
I cup sugar
4 eggs
I cup flour
I can chocolate syrup
½ cup chopped walnuts, *optional*

1. In a medium mixing bowl, use an electric mixer to cream the butter and sugar together.

2. Add the eggs one at a time and beat after each addition.

3. Stir in the flour, blending well.

4. Stir in the chocolate syrup, blending well.

5. Stir in the walnuts, if using.

6. Pour into a lightly greased 9-inch square baking pan.

7. Bake at 350°F for 25 to 30 minutes.

8. When cooled, cut into squares with a plastic knife. (A plastic knife won't drag crumbs while cutting.)

Pumpkin Pie Dessert

Bonnie Whaling, Clearfield, PA

Makes 4–6 servings

Prep. Time: 15–20 minutes ⚶ *Cooking Time: 3–4 hours* ⚶ *Ideal slow-cooker size: 5- to 6-qt.*

19-oz. can pumpkin pie filling

12-oz. can evaporated milk

2 eggs, lightly beaten

Boiling water

1 cup gingersnap cookie crumbs

1. In a large mixing bowl, stir together the pie filling, milk, and eggs until thoroughly mixed.

2. Pour into an ungreased baking insert designed to fit into your slow cooker.

3. Place the filled baking insert into the slow cooker. Cover the insert with its lid, or with 8 paper towels.

4. Carefully pour the boiling water into cooker around the baking insert, to a depth of 1 inch.

5. Cover the cooker. Cook on High for 3 to 4 hours, or until a tester inserted in the center of the custard comes out clean.

6. Remove the baking insert from the slow cooker. Remove its lid. Sprinkle the dessert with cookie crumbs. Serve warm from the baking insert.

Chocolate Chip Cheesecake

Chris Kaczynski, Schenectady, NY

Makes 16 servings

Prep. Time: 15 minutes ⚜ *Baking Time: 45–50 minutes* ⚜ *Chilling Time: 3–4 hours*

3 eggs, beaten

¾ cup sugar

3 8-oz. pkgs. cream cheese, softened

1 tsp. vanilla extract

24-oz. roll refrigerated chocolate chip cookie dough

1. Preheat the oven to 350°F.

2. Place all ingredients except the cookie dough in a large mixing bowl. With an electric mixer, blend together until creamy. Set aside.

3. Slice the cookie dough into ¼-inch-thick slices. Set aside 9 slices.

4. Lay the remaining slices in the bottom of a 9×13-inch baking pan. Pat the slices together to form a solid crust.

5. Spoon in the cream cheese mixture. Spread out over cookie crust.

6. Arrange the reserved nine cookie slices on top of the cream cheese mixture.

7. Bake at 350°F for 45 to 50 minutes. Allow to cool to room temperature.

8. Chill in the refrigerator. When firm, cut into squares.

9. If you wish, when serving, top with whipped cream or chocolate topping.

Cherry Cheesecake Tarts

Jan Mast, Lancaster, PA

Makes 18 servings

Prep. Time: 15 minutes ⚬ Baking Time: 15–20 minutes

18 vanilla wafers
8 oz. cream cheese, softened
3 eggs
¾ cup sugar
21-oz. can cherry pie filling

1. Fill 18 cupcake tins with paper cupcake liners.

2. Place 1 vanilla wafer in each paper liner. Set aside.

3. Beat the cream cheese just until soft and smooth. Do not overbeat.

4. Add the eggs and sugar to the beaten cream cheese, beating until just blended. Do not overbeat.

5. Pour the cream cheese mixture evenly into 18 cupcake liners, covering the vanilla wafers.

6. Bake at 325°F degrees for 15 to 20 minutes. Cool completely.

7. Top each cooled tart with cherry pie filling.

Tips:

1. Substitute blueberry pie filling or eliminate pie filling and use assorted fresh fruits, such as kiwi slices, orange slices, or strawberries.

2. Refrigerate after preparing.

3. Do not overbeat the cream cheese mixture— it needs to be heavy enough to keep the wafers at the bottom. If too much air is beaten into it, the wafers will float to the top.

Peanut Butter Fudge

Jamie Schwankl, Ephrata, PA

Makes 16 servings

Prep. Time: 10 minutes   Cooking Time: 5–8 minutes

2 sticks (16 Tbsp.) butter or margarine

1 tsp. vanilla extract

1 cup peanut butter

Pinch salt

3 cups confectioners' sugar

1. In a medium saucepan over low heat, melt the butter.

2. Add the vanilla, peanut butter, and salt. Mix with a spoon until smooth. Remove from the heat.

3. Add the confectioners' sugar. Stir until well blended.

4. Spread the mixture in an 8×8-inch pan to cool.

5. Refrigerate for 1 hour. Cut into small squares.

Tips:

1. A 7×9-inch pan also works well.

2. Do not use a mixer.

Snickers Apple Salad

Jennifer Archer, Kalona, IA

Makes 10–12 servings

Prep. Time: 15–20 minutes

3-oz. pkg. instant vanilla pudding

I cup milk

8 oz. frozen whipped topping, thawed

6 apples, peeled or unpeeled, diced

6 Snickers bars, diced or broken

1. In a large mixing bowl, mix the pudding mix with the milk.

2. Fold in the whipped topping.

3. Fold in the chopped apples and Snickers.

4. Cover and refrigerate until ready to serve.

Cookies-and-Cream Fluff

Ruth Hofstetter, Versailles, MO

Makes 6 servings

Prep. Time: 5–10 minutes

2 cups cold milk

3-oz. pkg. instant vanilla pudding mix

8 oz. frozen whipped topping, thawed

15 chocolate cream-filled sandwich cookies, broken into chunks

Additional broken cookies, *optional*

1. In a bowl, whisk the milk and pudding mix for 2 minutes, or until slightly thickened.

2. Fold in the whipped topping and cookies.

3. Spoon into dessert dishes.

4. When ready to serve, top with additional cookies if you wish.

Mandarin Orange Sherbet Dessert

CHILLED

Lori Lehman, Ephrata, PA
Mary Ann Bowman, East Earl, PA

Makes 8 servings

Prep. Time: 2 hours ⚬ *Chilling Time: 8 hours*

3-oz. pkg. orange gelatin
1 cup boiling water
1 pt. orange sherbet
16-oz. can mandarin oranges, drained
1 cup frozen whipped topping, thawed

1. Dissolve the gelatin in the boiling water. Place in a mixing bowl.

2. Add the sherbet and oranges. Place in the refrigerator until mixture begins to thicken, about 20 minutes.

3. Fold in the whipped topping.

4. Spoon into a serving dish. Cover and chill 8 hours before serving.

Variation:

Instead of folding the whipped topping into the dessert, use it as a topping just before serving.

—Mary Ann Bowman, East Earl, PA

Vanilla Pudding

Rhonda Freed, Croghan, NY

Makes 8–10 servings

Prep. Time: 15 minutes ❧ Cooking Time: 25 minutes ❧ Chilling Time: 2–4 hours

8 cups whole milk, *divided*
¾ cup cornstarch
1¼ cups sugar
2 eggs
2 tsp. vanilla extract

1. In a 3- or 4-qt. microwave-safe bowl, heat 6 cups milk in microwave on High until scalded, approximately 8 to 10 minutes.

2. Meanwhile, blend the remaining milk, cornstarch, sugar, and eggs in a blender until smooth.

3. Whisk the blended ingredients into the scalded milk.

4. Microwave on High for 5 minutes. Remove carefully with potholders and mix with a whisk.

5. Microwave on High for 4 minutes and stir. Decrease the cooking time by a minute each time until the pudding is a bit thinner than you want. (It will continue to thicken as it cools.)

6. Remove from the microwave. Stir in the vanilla.

7. While the pudding is still hot, cover with plastic wrap, pressing plastic against the surface of the pudding to prevent a skin from forming.

Variation:

Pour the finished pudding into ice pop molds. Freeze for pudding pops.

Caramel Custard

Nadine L. Martinitz, Salina, KS

Makes 8 servings

Prep. Time: 20 minutes ⚭ *Cooking/Baking Time: 40–45 minutes*
Standing/Cooling Time: 30 minutes–2 hours

1½ cups sugar, *divided*

6 eggs

2 tsp. vanilla extract

3 cups milk

1. In a heavy saucepan over low heat, cook and stir ¾ cup sugar just until melted and golden. Stir frequently to prevent burning.

2. Divide the caramelized sugar into eight 6-oz. custard cups. Tilt each cup after you've poured in the sugar to coat the bottom of the cup. Let stand for 10 minutes.

3. In a large mixing bowl, beat the eggs, vanilla, milk, and remaining sugar until combined but not foamy. Divide among the eight custard cups, pouring over the caramelized sugar.

4. Place the cups in two 8-inch square baking pans. Pour boiling water in pans to a depth of 1 inch.

5. Bake at 350°F for 40 to 45 minutes, or until a knife inserted in center of the custards comes out clean. Remove the cups from the pans to cool on wire racks.

6. To unmold, run a knife around the rim of each cup and invert the custard onto a dessert plate.

7. Serve warm or chilled.

Metric Equivalent Measurements

If you're accustomed to using metric measurements, I don't want you to be inconvenienced by the imperial measurements I use in this book.

Use this handy chart, too, to figure out the size of the slow cooker you'll need for each recipe.

Weight (Dry Ingredients)

1 oz		30 g
4 oz	¼ lb	120 g
8 oz	½ lb	240 g
12 oz	¾ lb	360 g
16 oz	1 lb	480 g
32 oz	2 lb	960 g

Slow Cooker Sizes

1-quart	0.96 l
2-quart	1.92 l
3-quart	2.88 l
4-quart	3.84 l
5-quart	4.80 l
6-quart	5.76 l
7-quart	6.72 l
8-quart	7.68 l

Volume (Liquid Ingredients)

½ tsp.		2 ml
1 tsp.		5 ml
1 Tbsp.	½ fl oz	15 ml
2 Tbsp.	1 fl oz	30 ml
¼ cup	2 fl oz	60 ml
⅓ cup	3 fl oz	80 ml
½ cup	4 fl oz	120 ml
⅔ cup	5 fl oz	160 ml
¾ cup	6 fl oz	180 ml
1 cup	8 fl oz	240 ml
1 pt	16 fl oz	480 ml
1 qt	32 fl oz	960 ml

Length

¼ in	6 mm
½ in	13 mm
¾ in	19 mm
1 in	25 mm
6 in	15 cm
12 in	30 cm

Recipe & Ingredient Index

About the Author

Hope Comerford is a mom, wife, elementary music teacher, blogger, recipe developer, public speaker, Young Living Essential Oils essential oil enthusiast/educator, and published author. In 2013, she was diagnosed with a severe gluten intolerance and since then has spent many hours creating easy, practical and delicious gluten-free recipes that can be enjoyed by both those who are affected by gluten and those who are not.

Growing up, Hope spent many hours in the kitchen with her Meme (grandmother), and her love for cooking grew from there. While working on her master's degree when her daughter was young, Hope turned to her slow cookers for some salvation and sanity. It was from there she began truly experimenting with recipes and quickly learned she had the ability to get a little more creative in the kitchen and develop her own recipes.

In 2010, Hope started her blog, *A Busy Mom's Slow Cooker Adventures*, to simply share the recipes she was making with her family and friends. She never imagined people all over the world would begin visiting her page and sharing her recipes with others as well. In 2013, Hope self-published her first cookbook, *Slow Cooker Recipes 10 Ingredients or Less and Gluten-Free*, and then later wrote *The Gluten-Free Slow Cooker*.

Hope became the new brand ambassador and author of Fix-It and Forget-It in mid-2016. Since then, she has brought her excitement and creativeness to the Fix-It and Forget-It brand. Through Fix-It and Forget-It, she has written *Fix-It and Forget-It Healthy Slow Cooker Cookbook*, *Fix-It and Forget-It Healthy 5-Ingredient Cookbook*, *Fix-It and Forget-It Instant Pot Cookbook*, *Fix-It and Forget-It Plant-Based Comfort Foods Cookbook*, *Welcome Home Harvest Cookbook*, *Welcome Home Pies, Crisps, and Crumbles*, and many more.

Hope lives in the city of Clinton Township, Michigan, near Metro Detroit. She has been happily married to her husband and best friend, Justin, since 2008. Together they have two children, Ella and Gavin, who are her motivation, inspiration, and heart. In her spare time, Hope enjoys traveling, singing, cooking, reading books, working on wooden puzzles, spending time with friends and family, and relaxing.